# The Intensified Glory Institute™

# SCHOOL OF SIGNS & WONDERS

## Course I

Published by
**New Wine International, Inc.**

Unless otherwise indicated, all scripture references are taken from the King James version of the Bible.

Where noted as NIV, scripture taken from the Holy Bible, New International Version ®. Copyright © 1973, 1978, 1984 by International Bible Society. Used by permission of Zondervan. All rights reserved.

Where noted as AMP, scripture quotations taken from the Amplified ® Bible. Copyright © 1954, 1958, 1962, 1964, 1965, 1987 by The Lockman Foundation. Used by permission.

**THE INTENSIFIED GLORY INSTITUTE™**
School of Signs & Wonders
ISBN 978-0-578-01053-3
Copyright © MMIX by Joshua Mills

*Published by*
**New Wine International, Inc.**
www.NewWineInternational.org

Printed in the United States of America.

# SCHOOL OF SIGNS & WONDERS

## WITH JOSHUA MILLS

### COURSE I - TABLE OF CONTENTS

## X    HOW TO RECEIVE BLESSING, FAVOR & INCREASE  221-240

## XI    POWER IN YOUR HANDS                    241-254

www.IntensifiedGloryInstitute.com

**THE INTENSIFIED GLORY INSTITUTE DISCLAIMER:**

We walk by revelation, and the Lord has taught us to keep an open spirit to the new things He is doing. We walk softly before God, and do not pretend to be authorities on everything that God is doing. We see in part and we prophesy in part. Therefore, through this course we are sharing with you tidbits of revelation that we have received as we've ministered through signs and wonders around the world. The teaching contained within this manual is only intended to be a launching point for you to go deeper into the things of the Spirit. The Lord may show you something slightly different or you may discount something entirely. The only infallible Word is the Word of God which is contained within the holy scriptures (2 Timothy 3:16).

This training manual is not intended to provide medical advice or to take the place of medical advice and treatment from your personal physician. Students are advised to consult their own doctors or other qualified health professionals regarding the treatment of their medical problems. Neither the publisher nor the author takes any responsibility for any possible consequences from any treatment, action, or medical application to any person reading or following the information in this book. If students are taking prescription medications, they should consult with their physicians and not take themselves off of medicines without the proper supervision of a physician.

# Welcome to
# THE INTENSIFIED GLORY INSTITUTE

*"Study to show thyself approved unto God, a workman that need not be ashamed, rightly dividing the word of truth."*
– II Timothy 2:15

It is our joy and honor to welcome you to the Intensified Glory Institute. We know that you are here because you are hungry for more of God's Word and the revelation that only comes by the Spirit of glory.

We believe that God has led you here to be "taught of the Lord." This training and equipping school is a result of many hours of prayer, diligent research in the Word and practical ministry experience. For quite a few years now we have been feeling the prompting of the Lord to facilitate a school where we could release teaching and impartation that would allow the message of God's glory to multiply in the hearts and spirits of the students. A school where Jesus Christ would be glorified and His gospel of miracle-working power would be preached. That school is the **Intensified Glory Institute**.

Prepare to learn, prepare to be challenged, prepare to experience new realms of glory, prepare to receive impartation and prepare to be blessed!

We know that through the impartation you will receive at this school, you will be equipped with the necessary tools to become a powerful wonderworker and laborer in the greatest harvest of souls the earth has ever known.

Welcome to the **Intensified Glory Institute** family!

In His Great Love,

*Joshua & Janet Angela Mills*

Joshua & Janet Angela Mills

10

The Intensified Glory Institute
School of Signs & Wonders

**Lesson #1**
# THREE REALMS OF THE SUPERNATURAL

## Course I – Lesson 1

## THREE REALMS OF THE SUPERNATURAL

**Objective:** To understand the three realms of the spirit that God has made available to each and every believer, and how they can be activated to access the glory realm.

**Overview:** Within this lesson we will search the scriptures and find out what the Word of God says about the three realms of the supernatural:

- Understanding The Three Realms

- Facts About Faith

- What Is The Anointing?

- 3 Kinds Of Anointings

- What Is The Glory?

- What Does The Glory Look Like?

- The Test For All Supernatural Experiences

**SCRIPTURES FOR MEDITATION:**

☐ Hebrews 11:1-6

☐ Romans 1:17

☐ Acts 2

☐ Isaiah 60:1-5

☐ Haggai 2:1-9

## HIDDEN REVELATION

## UNDERSTANDING THE THREE REALMS

Many times within the scriptures we find that God works in threes:

_____

_____

_____

_____

_____

_____

_____

_____

There are three realms in the spirit:

    1. _____

    2. _____

    3. _____

There are three realms within mankind:

    1. _____

    2. _____

    3. _____

Each realm builds upon the one before. God is building and establishing something inside of us that comes step by step.

The Intensified Glory Institute ———————— NOTES

*"And all of us, as with unveiled face, continued to behold as in a mirror the glory of the Lord, are constantly being transfigured into His very own image in ever increasing splendor and from one degree of glory to another; for this comes from the Lord who is the Spirit."* – 2 Corinthians 3:18 (AMP)

In order to enter into the realms of God's glory we must begin in the area of faith.

Faith is the _____ for all spiritual experiences.

## FACTS ABOUT FAITH

- Hebrews 11:6 – We cannot _____ God without it.

- 1 John 5:4 – Faith always releases the power for _____!

- Romans 4:16-25 – It is _____

- Galatians 5:6 – Faith works by _____

- Hebrews 11:1 – Faith is the _____ of things hoped for, the _____ of things not seen.

| Faith is always spelled as | |
|---|---|
| | |
| | |
| | |
| | |

www.IntensifiedGloryInstitute.com

## FAITH & SPIRITUAL SENSES

Faith creates realms of possibility and opens doors for the invisible realm to be made manifest in the natural. We walk by faith and not by sight – but as we walk by faith, we begin to see through eyes of faith. Faith activates our spiritual senses and causes them to come alive:

1. **Faith _____**

   *"So then faith cometh by hearing, and hearing by the word of God."*
   Romans 10:17

2. **Faith _____**

   *"I will stand upon my watch, and set me upon the tower, and will watch to see what he will say unto me, and what I shall answer when I am reproved. And the LORD answered me, and said, Write the vision, and make it plain upon tables, that he may run that readeth it. For the vision is yet for an appointed time, but at the end it shall speak, and not lie: though it tarry, wait for it; because it will surely come, it will not tarry."*
   Habakkuk 2:1-3

3. **Faith _____**

   *"But what saith it? The word is nigh thee, even in thy mouth, and in thy heart: that is, the word of faith, which we preach; That if thou shalt confess with thy mouth the Lord Jesus, and shalt believe in thine heart that God hath raised him from the dead, thou shalt be saved. For with the heart man believeth unto righteousness; and with the mouth confession is made unto salvation."* – Romans 10:8-10

4. **Faith _____**

   *"O taste and see that the LORD is good: blessed is the man that trusteth in him."* – Psalm 34:8

*"A little faith will bring your soul to heaven, but a lot of faith will bring heaven to your soul."* – **Dwight L. Moody**

5. **Faith** _____

*"Be careful for nothing; but in everything by prayer and supplication with thanksgiving let your requests be made known unto God."*
Philippians 4:6

6. **Faith** _____

*"But be ye doers of the word, and not hearers only, deceiving your own selves."* – James 1:22

*"For as the body without the spirit is dead, so faith without works is dead also."* – James 2:26

7. **Faith** _____

*"And let us not be weary in well doing: for in due season we shall reap, if we faint not."* – Galatians 6:9

8. **Faith** _____

*"Therefore I say unto you, What things soever ye desire, when ye pray, believe that ye receive them, and ye shall have them."* – Mark 11:24

## THE PURPOSE OF OUR FAITH

We must have faith in:

- **God's Word**

*"And that from a child thou hast known the holy scriptures, which are able to make thee wise unto salvation through faith which is in Christ Jesus. All scripture is given by inspiration of God, and is profitable for*

*doctrine, for reproof, for correction, for instruction in righteousness: That the man of God may be perfect, thoroughly furnished unto all good works."* – 2 Timothy 3:15-17

- **Salvation through Jesus Christ**

*"That if thou shalt confess with thy mouth the Lord Jesus, and shalt believe in thine heart that God hath raised him from the dead, thou shalt be saved. For with the heart man believeth unto righteousness; and with the mouth confession is made unto salvation."* – Romans 10:9-10

- **The Supernatural Power of God**

*"Blessed be the God and Father of our Lord Jesus Christ, which according to his abundant mercy hath begotten us again unto a lively hope by the resurrection of Jesus Christ from the dead, To an inheritance incorruptible, and undefiled, and that fadeth not away, reserved in heaven for you, Who are kept by the power of God through faith unto salvation ready to be revealed in the last time."* – 1 Peter 1:3-5

## WHAT IS THE ANOINTING?

*"The Spirit of the Lord is upon me, because He has anointed me to preach the good news to the poor; He has sent me to announce release to the captives and recovery of sight to the blind, to send forth as delivered those who are oppressed, to proclaim the accepted and acceptable year of the Lord."* – Luke 4:18-19

1. It is the _____ of God that sets us apart.

2. It allows the _____ of the _____ to function freely. It is a divine enablement for us to accomplish God's supernatural purposes here on earth.

3. It brings _____ and _____. The anointing gives us power for obstacles and the ability to overcome problems.

*"… the yoke shall be destroyed because of the anointing."* – Isaiah 10:27

The Intensified Glory Institute ———————— NOTES

In the Old Testament they would anoint Kings, Priests and Prophets with anointing oil in order for them to take their position and do *the job*.

*"Then shalt thou take the anointing oil, and pour it upon his head, and anoint him."* – Exodus 29:7

- Priests – Psalm 133:2

- Kings – 1 Samuel 16:3, 2 Samuel 2:4, 1 Kings 19:15

- Prophets – 1 Kings 19:16, Psalm 105:15

The word "anoint" means to "_____ _____" or "_____ _____"

Today the Holy Spirit anoints believers so that we will take our rightful position in Christ and begin to do *the job*.

The anointing comes to equip and protect the entire body of Christ:

*"…Touch not mine anointed, and do my prophets no harm."* – Psalm 105:15

The anointing establishes us in fellowship with one another:

*"Now he which establisheth us with you in Christ, and hath anointed us, is God."* – 2 Corinthians 1:21

The anointing will teach you and give you supernatural abilities which you do not have in the natural realm:

*"But ye have an unction from the Holy One, and ye know all things… But the anointing which ye have received of him abideth in you, and ye need not that any man teach you: but as the same anointing teacheth you of all things, and is truth, and is no lie, and even as it hath taught you, ye shall abide in him."*
- 1 John 2:20,27

The Intensified Glory Institute ——————— NOTES

## THREE KINDS OF ANOINTINGS

1. **Anointing with** _____ (Genesis 28:18, Mark 6:7-13)

2. **Compound Of** _____ (Exodus 30:22-25)

3. _____ _____ (Psalm 45:7, Isaiah 61:1, Luke 4:18-21, Acts 10:38, Hebrews 1:9)

God allows us to be anointed so that we can do the supernatural works of Jesus Christ. We use the realms of faith and anointing to release the glory of God.

- The anointing _____ us – we swim in the River of God.

- The glory _____ us – we surf on the waves of His flow.

*"Let us labour therefore to enter into that rest..."* – Hebrews 4:11

The Intensified Glory Institute ——————— NOTES

## WHAT IS THE GLORY?

God is the glory, and the glory is God!

God's glory is His manifest shekinah.  It is His character, His nature, His ability and provision, the weight and splendor of His majesty – it is the essence of His presence.  His glory is all that He is and all that He does!

The glory of God is the realm of rest.  There is an ease in the glory.

*"Arise, shine; for thy light is come, and the glory of the LORD is risen upon thee.  For, behold, the darkness shall cover the earth, and gross darkness the people: but the LORD shall arise upon thee, and his glory shall be seen upon thee.  And the Gentiles shall come to thy light, and kings to the brightness of thy rising.  Lift up thine eyes round about, and see…"* – Isaiah 60:1-4

- The glory causes us to shine with the brilliance of the heavens.

- The glory increases our witness and influence.  The glory draws people unto the *"brightness of our rising"*.

- The glory changes our perspective and causes us to look "up" to see.

*"Then thou shalt see, and flow together, and thine heart shall fear, and be enlarged; because the abundance of the sea shall be converted unto thee, the forces of the Gentiles shall come unto thee.  The multitude of camels shall cover thee, the dromedaries of Midian and Ephah; all they from Sheba shall come: they shall bring gold and incense; and they shall shew forth the praises of the LORD.  All the flocks of Kedar shall be gathered together unto thee, the rams of Nebaioth shall minister unto thee: they shall come up with acceptance on mine altar, and I will glorify the house of my glory."* – Isaiah 60:5-7

- The glory brings harvest and finances.

- The glory causes praise and worship to arise.

- The Lord says "I will glorify the house of my glory."

The Intensified Glory Institute ———————————— NOTES

*"Your gates will always stand open, they will never be shut, day or night, so that men may bring you the wealth of the nations— their kings led in triumphal procession."* – Isaiah 60:11 (NIV)

- The glory opens up doors that cannot be shut

## WHAT DOES THE GLORY LOOK LIKE?

- **A Thick Cloud**
  Exodus 16:10
  Exodus 19:9
  2 Chronicles 5:13-14

- **Fire & Light**
  Exodus 3:2
  Exodus 24:17
  Isaiah 60:1

- **Shimmering Brilliance**
  Ezekiel 1:27-28

- **Manna & Provision**
  Exodus 16:4-31
  Matthew 16:8-10
  Philippians 4:19

- **Supernatural Dew**
  Judges 6:36-40

Throughout this school, we will begin to explore the different aspects and dimensions of God's glory as it is released through signs and wonders.

## HOW HAVE YOU SEEN THE GLORY?

Use these next few lines to describe ways that you've seen the glory of God manifest around you.

- _____

- _____

- _____

 **KEYS FOR ACTIVATION**

## THE TEST FOR ALL SUPERNATURAL EXPERIENCES

### 1. The Word of God

If the experience or "miracle" contradicts the Bible, stay clear of it. Everything that Jesus Christ does today through the work of the Holy Spirit will come in line with the Word and be consistent with the holy scriptures. All of our spiritual experiences must have their foundations in the Word of God.

Isaiah 55:11          Matthew 24:35          John 17:17
Romans 4:17          Ephesians 1:3          Hebrews 11:3

### 2. Is Jesus Christ glorified through the experience?

Jesus is the Word and the Word is God. If the experience lowers Jesus Christ from His position of Godhead, stay clear of it. God, the Father, receives glory through His Son, Jesus Christ. A "sign" should make you "wonder" – it should point you to Jesus Christ, the Wonder of Wonders!

John 1:1
Romans 16:27

### 3. The Message of the Cross.

Redemption is not by good works but through the finished work of Jesus Christ on the cross of Calvary. We are redeemed because of the blood and atonement of Jesus Christ.

Revelation 5:8-10
John 14:6
Hebrews 9:14

## RECOMMENDED RESOURCES:

*CDs*

### Carry Your Climate
By Joshua Mills
Released by PIP Media Group
P.O. Box 4037, Palm Springs, CA 92263

*Books*

### The Fourth Dimension
By Dr. David Yonggi Cho
Published Bridge-Logos Publishers
Alachua, Florida 32615

### Glory: Experiencing The Atmosphere Of Heaven
By Ruth Ward Heflin
Published by McDougal Publishing
P.O. Box 3595, Hagerstown, MD 21742

All resources are available online at:
www.NewWineInternational.org

# The Intensified Glory Institute
# School of Signs & Wonders

## Lesson #2
## HOW TO HEAR GOD'S VOICE

## Course I – Lesson 2

## HOW TO HEAR GOD'S VOICE

**Objective:** To understand what God's voice sounds like when He speaks, and how to understand what He is saying to us.

**Overview:** Within this lesson we will search the scriptures and find out what the Word of God says about hearing the voice of the Lord.

- Does Every Christian Hear The Voice Of God?

- How Does God Speak?

- The Mind Of Christ

- The Seven Spirits Of God

## SCRIPTURES FOR MEDITATION:

☐ Jeremiah 7:23-24

☐ Psalm 25:9

☐ John 10:14

☐ John 15:7-12

☐ John 16:12-15

☐ Romans 8:14

www.IntensifiedGloryInstitute.com

The Intensified Glory Institute ———————— NOTES

## HIDDEN REVELATION

## DOES EVERY CHRISTIAN HEAR THE VOICE OF GOD?

*"I am the Good Shepherd; and I know and recognize My own, and My own know and recognize Me."* – John 10:14 (AMP)

*"No man can come to me, except the Father which hath sent me draw him: and I will raise him up at the last day. It is written in the prophets, And they shall be all taught of God. Every man therefore that hath heard, and hath learned of the Father, cometh unto me."* – John 6:44-45

"Does every Christian hear the voice of God?" The answer to this question is YES! Every Christian hears God's voice. The scripture in John 6 explains that it is only by the voice of God, the Father, that we were drawn unto the person of Jesus Christ to receive salvation through Him.

It was God's voice that drew us unto Himself. And His voice will continue to lead us in this walk of faith. If you've heard His voice once, you can hear it again! The more you become familiar with His voice, the more you'll recognize it – even when He's speaking very softly.

## HOW DOES GOD SPEAK?

*"He that is of God heareth God's words…"* – John 8:47

God will speak to us in several ways:

1. **Through His _____** (2 Timothy 3:16-17)

2. **Through Other _____** (Amos 3:7, 1 Corinthians 14:31)

3. **Through the _____ _____** (Romans 8:14)

The Intensified Glory Institute ——————————— NOTES

*What Does The Voice Of The Holy Spirit Sound Like?*

1. _____   2. _____

3. _____   4. _____

5. _____   6. _____

## THE MIND OF CHRIST

*"Which things also we speak, not in the words which man's wisdom teacheth, but which the Holy Ghost teacheth; comparing spiritual things with spiritual. But the natural man receiveth not the things of the Spirit of God: for they are foolishness unto him: neither can he know them, because they are spiritually discerned. But he that is spiritual judgeth all things, yet he himself is judged of no man. For who hath known the mind of the Lord, that he may instruct him? but we have the mind of Christ."* – 1 Corinthians 2:13-16

We do not hear God's voice through our own intellect – but God chooses to speak to us through the person of the Holy Spirit. HE is the mind of Christ and WE have the mind of Christ.

*"I have yet many things to say unto you, but ye cannot bear them now. Howbeit when he, the Spirit of truth, is come, he will guide you into all truth: for he shall not speak of himself; but whatsoever he shall hear, that shall he speak: and he will shew you things to come. He shall glorify me: for he shall receive of mine, and shall shew it unto you. All things that the Father hath are mine: therefore said I, that he shall take of mine, and shall shew it unto you."* – John 16:12-15

God connects with us Spirit to spirit.

We can have access to the will of God, the thoughts of God and the emotions of God. We are to be guided by the Holy Spirit (the Spirit of truth) who communicates to us things that are many times too deep for human language. This is why we will often "sense" what God is saying through our thoughts or our feelings.

The Intensified Glory Institute ———————————— NOTES

Jesus Christ prayed for the Father to send us the Holy Spirit that we would not be alone, but so that we would have the Spirit of truth with us at all times.

*"And I will pray the Father, and he shall give you another Comforter, that he may abide with you forever; Even the Spirit of truth; whom the world cannot receive, because it seeth him not, neither knoweth him: but ye know him; for he dwelleth with you, and shall be in you."* – John 14:16-17

The Holy Spirit will begin to reveal "God thoughts" or "God emotions" to us as He dwells with us.

## THE SEVEN SPIRITS OF GOD

*"And the spirit of the LORD shall rest upon him, the spirit of wisdom and understanding, the spirit of counsel and might, the spirit of knowledge and of the fear of the LORD; And shall make him of quick understanding in the fear of the LORD: and he shall not judge after the sight of his eyes, neither reprove after the hearing of his ears."* – Isaiah 11:2-3

By faith, begin declaring that the Seven Spirits of God are <u>resting upon you</u> and <u>releasing a supernatural understanding</u> – so that you will not walk by the sight of your natural eyes, or the sound of your natural ears, but that you would begin walking in the Spirit of God with the mind of Christ.

The Intensified Glory Institute ———————————— NOTES

 **KEYS FOR ACTIVATION**

**Key Verse:**_____

**KEY #1**

**KEY #2**

**KEY #3**

**KEY #4**

The Intensified Glory Institute ———————————— NOTES

**APPLICATIONS FOR HOME**

1. Set time aside each day – or at least each week – to be in a place where you can focus on listening to the "God thoughts" and images which are going through your mind.

   - Write these thoughts down, or record them in some way.

   - Ask God to increase the revelation.

   - Pray for each of the "Seven Spirits Of God" to be made manifest in your thought life.

   *"But thou, when thou prayest, enter into thy closet, and when thou hast shut thy door, pray to thy Father which is in secret; and thy Father which seeth in secret shall reward thee openly."* – Matthew 6:6

2. Every month take time to look over your journal entries, and allow the Spirit of God to put together these pieces of the puzzle. As you do this, you will begin to discover bigger pictures and gain greater understanding of what God is saying to you.

   *"Being confident of this very thing, that he which hath begun a good work in you will perform it until the day of Jesus Christ"* – Philippians 1:6

3. When you begin to listen for the voice of God, here are some great practical questions to ask yourself about the revelations you're receiving:

   - Does it line up with the scriptures?

   - Does it lead you into a closer relationship with God?

   - Is this revelation leading you into expressing the love of God? Putting God's benefit and the benefit of others before your own benefit?

- Does it cause greater love, joy and peace from God in you?

*"But he that entereth in by the door is the shepherd of the sheep. To him the porter openeth; and the sheep hear his voice: and he calleth his own sheep by name, and leadeth them out. And when he putteth forth his own sheep, he goeth before them, and the sheep follow him: for they know his voice. And a stranger will they not follow, but will flee from him: for they know not the voice of strangers."* – John 10:2-5

# The Intensified Glory Institute
# School of Signs & Wonders

## Lesson #3
## THIRD DAY INTERCESSION

**Course I - Lesson 3**

**THIRD DAY INTERCESSION**

**Objective:** To become familiar with third day intercession and praying in the spirit. Through this teaching students will begin to understand the important role that prayer plays in the life of every believer.

**Overview:** Within this lesson we will search the scriptures and find out what the Word of God says about third day intercession:

- What Is Intercession?

- Understanding "The Now"

- Revelation Always Brings Manifestation

- Praying In The Spirit

- Responding To The Realm Through Prophetic Acts

- The Difference Between Pressing In & Entering In

- An Outline For Third Day Intercession

- Intercessory Lifestyle

- Declaring The Glory!

## SCRIPTURES FOR MEDITATION:

☐ Acts 4:31

☐ Isaiah 55:11

☐ Romans 8:26

☐ Hebrews 11

The Intensified Glory Institute —————————— NOTES

 **HIDDEN REVELATION**

## WHAT IS INTERCESSION?

Intercession is the act of prayer, petition, or entreaty in favor of another or others.

In the bible we can see two examples of prophetic intercession:
- Foretelling in the _____ _____
- Forthtelling in the _____ _____

1.  First and second day intercession speaks to the things ___ _____.
    a. confession

*Foretelling* is prophesying a future event or things to come.  *Foretelling* prophesies things *into the future*.

2. Third day intercession is prophetic and speaks to the things _____ ____ _____.
    a. declaration
    b. speaking it NOW!

*Forthtelling* is prophesying and declaring something into the now.
*Forthtelling* prophesies and *moves the future into today*!

**As a Third Day Intercessor you will:**

1. Carry a Prophetic Voice

2. Change the Atmosphere Through Prayer

3. See into the realm of the Spirit

4. Move things from Heaven to Earth

5. Speak God's **NOW** Word !  *Forthtell* the things of God!

www.IntensifiedGloryInstitute.com

The Intensified Glory Institute ——————— NOTES

## GOD NEEDS FAITHFUL INTERCESSORS

God is looking for faithful intercessors.

*"The LORD looked down from heaven upon the children of men, to see if there were any that did understand, and seek God."* – Psalm 14:2

*"For the eyes of the LORD run to and fro throughout the whole earth, to shew himself strong in the behalf of them whose heart is perfect toward him."*
– 2 Chronicles 16:9

God is seeking those who will be faithful and keep their hearts perfect towards Him. He is looking for those intercessors that will birth forth His heavenly plans into the earthly realm.

When God is about to do something new He lays new spiritual foundations, because you can't put new wine into old wineskins.

*"According to the grace of God which is given unto me, as a wise masterbuilder, I have laid the foundation, and another buildeth thereon. But let every man take heed how he buildeth thereupon."* – 1 Corinthians 3:10

Paul said that a foundation is being laid and we need to be careful how we build on it. You can't put something stale with something fresh because it will spoil the newness of it. In this move of God's glory we need to recognize the flow and allow God to place His mind within us.

We can't allow old mindsets and traditions to spoil the freshness of this flow. In the glory we move past warfare into worship. We rise above the battle and rest in the blessing!

Pray until you go where you have never gone before.

Praise and declare your future into the now!

The Intensified Glory Institute ———————————— NOTES

# UNDERSTANDING "THE NOW"

It's important that we believe in the **NOW**. We need to start speaking to the **NOW**. We need to stop putting all of our hope into the future. Speak it **NOW**.

*"…behold, now is the accepted time; behold, now is the day of salvation."*
– 2 Corinthians 6:2

There is no moment like **NOW**. In Hebrews 11, the bible declares that *"**NOW** FAITH IS the substance of things hoped for, the evidence of things not seen."*

As you intercede and pray, begin to speak things into the **NOW**. Prophesy them **NOW**. Speak and declare what you hear the Lord saying.

Faith filled words will put you over. Fear filled words will defeat you.
Your words are the most powerful thing in the universe.

*Your words contain the power to create the worlds that you will walk into tomorrow. Your future is contained within the words you speak today!*

● Your voice is _____ (Proverbs 6:1-2, Proverbs 18:21)

● Your voice will bring forth the _____ of God's glory. (Jeremiah 1:12)

● Begin to speak *"those things that are not, as if they were."* (Romans 4:17)

The Intensified Glory Institute ───────────── NOTES

# REVELATION ALWAYS BRINGS MANIFESTATION

*When we sow words of revelation, we will see a harvest of manifestation!*

1. God shows it, we speak it, and it happens!

*"Surely the Sovereign LORD does nothing without revealing his plan to his servants the prophets."* – Amos 3:7 (NIV)

2. The Word of God is life and manifests in the same way

*"My son, attend to my words; incline thine ear unto my sayings. Let them not depart from thine eyes; keep them in the midst of thine heart. For they are life unto those that find them, and health to all their flesh."* – Proverbs 4:20-22

3. We will reap what we have sown in intercession

*"Be not deceived; God is not mocked: for whatsoever a man soweth, that shall he also reap."* – Galatians 6:7

As you begin to intercede in prayer, it is vital that you hear from heaven and declare with your mouth that which you hear.

## CORPORATE THIRD DAY INTERCESSION

What happens in a meeting, conference, or other corporate gathering of believers is the result of what has happened in times of intercession before the meeting.

Whatever is prophesied during intercessory prayer will happen.

This is why our intercession is so important to set the atmosphere for what God wants to do. We will declare it in our intercession to see God bring it forth in the glory realm.

The Intensified Glory Institute —————————— NOTES

As you pray and intercede for the requests of those around you, hear from heaven and begin speaking God's purposes and will into every situation. SPEAK THE THINGS OF HEAVEN NOW!

**Every new revelation from God will bring you into a new elevation in God!**

As you begin stepping out in this form of intercession, you will learn many things as the Holy Spirit is your teacher – He promises to teach you and guide you into all truth. You will be ignited and alerted to see how God demonstrates and confirms the spoken rhema word.

*"So shall My word be that goes forth out of My mouth: it shall not return to Me void [without producing any effect, useless], but it shall accomplish that which I please and purpose, and it shall prosper in the thing for which I sent it."*
– Isaiah 55:11 (AMP)

**God's Word always prospers – if it's alive inside of you, you will prosper too!**

*"Humble yourselves in the sight of the Lord, and he shall lift you up."*
– James 4:10

*"For promotion cometh neither from the east, nor from the west, nor from the south. But God is the judge: he putteth down one, and setteth up another."*
– Psalm 75:6-7

**If you promote the Word of God – the Word of God will promote you!**

The Intensified Glory Institute ———————— NOTES

# PRAYING IN THE SPIRIT

*"So too the [Holy] Spirit comes to our aid and bears us up in our weakness; for we do not know what prayer to offer nor how to offer it worthily as we ought, but the Spirit Himself goes to meet our supplication and pleads in our behalf with unspeakable yearnings and groanings too deep for utterance."* – Romans 8:26

Praying in the Spirit builds you up spirit, soul and body.

When you pray in the Spirit, you always pray past where you have been. It might seem like you are just doing your duty in the spirit, however, you are activating and creating something that is going on in the realm of the glory. By praying in the Spirit you're bringing your prayers from eternity into time – moving them from heaven to earth.

One of the greatest revelations of the Spirit is that something is always happening in the glory realm. The activity of heaven is always moving. The Angels, the flashing lightning from the throne, the whirlwinds of God are moving. Every time we pray in the Spirit, something is moving from heaven to earth into our spirit man.

- Pray past where you are

- Pray past where you have been

- Pray in the Spirit!

# RESPONDING TO THE REALM THROUGH PROPHETIC ACTS

In third day intercession, we see into the Spirit realm and we act upon what we see. We respond to the realm of glory in this way. If we wait for "feelings" or what we "feel like doing" – then many times it's too late! **A Watchman always needs to be alert and on the look out!**

The Intensified Glory Institute —————————— NOTES

In Third Day Intercession We Simply:

1. _____

2. _____

3. _____ *(Respond)*

Be prayerful – keep your eyes open to see what God is doing and act upon the revelation. As intercessors we will lead others into responding and receiving from the realm.

*A "Third Day Intercessor" will see it first, say it first and do it first!*

From experience I have found that we have an approximate 30-40 second window of opportunity to respond to the realm when the Holy Spirit shows us something.

I like to encourage people to lift their hands into the heavens and pray in the Holy Ghost. It is a prophetic act.

Through these prophetic acts we are taking of the physical and placing it into the supernatural that we see in the Spirit. It moves us into the glory.

Examples:

- When we see a brand new door of opportunity opening in the Spirit, we can act prophetically by taking a "step into it" in the natural.

- If the miracle realm comes for healing, we can stand in it.

- If the miracle realm comes for restoration, we can pull it down.

- If the miracle realm comes for finances, we can give into it. It is possible to sow financial seed into a spoken word as a prophetic act of faith.

- If the praise realm comes, we're the first to dance, jump and shout!

We need to learn how to pray, see and act!

Other people will follow your actions – so "Third Day Intercessors" learn how to act on the Word and respond to the glory realm.

## THE DIFFERENCE BETWEEN "PRESSING IN" & "ENTERING IN"

It is important for us to learn the difference between pressing in and entering in.

- In the anointing we press in.

The reason why we press in under the anointing is because that is what empowers us to stay in the glory. The more we press in, the greater the flow – the greater the manifestation of God's presence.

You press in to soar. The eagle flaps his wings to rise above the currents, but once he rises to that height then he just glides. There is rest in the glory of God. Third day intercession will bring you into the rest.

- In the glory we enter in.

This comes with ease. We enter in to receive the fullness and benefits of the realm and all that is being released from the heavenlies. We STAND in the glory!

**KEYS FOR ACTIVATION**

THE NEW WINE
# G.R.A.P.E.
*AN OUTLINE FOR THIRD DAY INTERCESSION*

**G**ive            Luke 6:38

**R**elease       Matthew 16:19

**A**noint        Isaiah 10:27

**P**ray           1 Thessalonians 5:17

**E**xcel         Jeremiah 29:11

**G**ive... Give God the glory in advance for what He is doing. Give Him praise and worship. Give of yourself to God through prayer and devotion. As you pray and intercede write down your thoughts, feelings, words, visions, etc. This way you can give it to the body of Christ. It is good to write it down and sent it to us through the post or email. Give of your time and efforts through volunteering in a ministry position. Give financially to the ministry of New Wine International, and sow into the glory realm as the Lord directs.

**R**elease... Release the people in the local area and around the world to come to the meetings. Release salvations. Release miracles, signs and wonders. Release revelation. Release finances. Release new sounds and heavenly worship. Release the Angelic host of heaven.

www.IntensifiedGloryInstitute.com

**A**noint... Anoint this ministry with the oil of the Holy Spirit as you pray and intercede. Anoint the worship. Anoint the Word of God that will be spoken. Anoint Joshua & Janet Angela Mills or other ministry leaders. Anoint the office staff. Anoint other Pastors and leadership team. Anoint the ministry of helps – the sound, the worship team, the workers and volunteers, etc.

**P**ray... Pray for Israel. Pray for your nation and the nations of the world. Pray for those in authority. Keep Joshua & Janet Angela Mills and their family covered in prayer. Pray the blood of Jesus Christ over them, their home, their family, and every church where they minister. Pray in the Spirit for those who will sit under their ministry – that they may have spiritual ears to hear, and eyes to see what the Holy Spirit is doing.

**E**xcel... Excel in the glory realm. Let the Lord take you up into higher and new realms as you intercede. Watch your tongue. Avoid all gossip and careless talking, which will cause you to lose your focus (and it will bring you down). God is calling you UP in the things of the glory. You WILL excel in your intercession. Excel in the things of the Spirit – allow Him to take you to new places in your times of prayer and intercession.

The Intensified Glory Institute —————————— NOTES

 **APPLICATIONS FOR HOME**

## 1. INTERCESSORY LIFESTYLE

This type of third day intercession can become a lifestyle! Stay in the Spirit and begin living from that realm.

**PRAYER IS WHAT YOU DO
BECAUSE IT'S WHO YOU ARE!**

*"Even them will I bring to my holy mountain, and make them joyful in my house of prayer: their burnt offerings and their sacrifices shall be accepted upon mine altar; for mine house shall be called an house of prayer for all people."*
– Isaiah 56:7

*"Rejoice evermore. Pray without ceasing. In everything give thanks: for this is the will of God in Christ Jesus concerning you."* – 1 Thessalonians 5:16-18

## 2. DO THE NEW WINE "GRAPE" ON A DAILY BASIS AND BEGIN DECLARING THE GLORY!

You can begin actively declaring and releasing these statements over the following areas of your life:
- Home
- Family
- Church / Ministry
- Community
- Nation

The Intensified Glory Institute ———————————— NOTES

## DECLARING THE GLORY!

**The righteous shall rule, they shall reign!**
**As it is in heaven –**

There is victory in heaven; There is wonder working power in heaven;
There is joy and peace in heaven; There is freedom in heaven;
The Lord reigns in heaven;

**So as it is in heaven, we loose it on earth!**

We loose abundance!  We loose prosperity, we loose heavenly riches!
We loose faith and hope!  We loose love!
We loose the Holy Ghost and Fire!

**The righteous shall rule!  They shall reign!**

We loose life everlasting through the Blood of the Lamb!
We loose sound minds!  We loose new hearts!
We loose the gifts of the Spirit!
We loose the breath of God and we say that these dry bones shall live!
It's beginning to rain, and at the smell of water, these bones shall live!
We loose our inheritance!
For in heaven, the Lord was, is and shall be – all at the same time!

**The righteous shall rule!  They shall reign!**

We declare freedom to the captives; Opening of the eyes of the blind;
The lame shall walk and leap as a lark!
We declare all God's children in peace and harmony!

**As it is in heaven, we loose it on the earth.**
**The righteous shall rule!  They shall reign!**

We loose righteousness and holiness; We loose self-control;

We loose humility and banish pride; We bind lasciviousness and loose purity!

**As it is in heaven, we loose it on earth:**

We loose unity! We loose harmony! We loose the heavenly language!
And, we loose the songs of heaven!

**As it is in heaven, we loose it on earth.**

We loose our authority; We loose our dominion;
We loose our kingships and our lordships;
For the Lord is King of kings and Lord of lords!

**The righteous shall rule, they shall reign.**

We loose the plans and purposes of God; We loose our destiny;
We loose good cheer; We loose the spirit of the warrior.

**As it is in heaven, we loose it on earth!**

He is treading down the vintage! We loose war on wickedness!
We tread upon serpents and scorpions! We bind all lies and loose the truth!

**As it is in heaven, we loose it on earth.**

We loose the sounds of heaven; We loose the victory cry!
We loose intimacy with our Bridegroom;
We loose the sanctity of marriage upon the earth;
We bind perverseness and we loose chastity.
We loose the washing of the water by the Word;
We loose the River of God to flow with life changing currents.
We loose the horses; We loose strength and power! We loose honor and glory!

**As it is in heaven, we loose it on earth!**

We loose sanctification and justification on the saints;
We loose the spirit of conviction on the sinners;
We loose submission to authority; We loose understanding and wisdom;

**As it is in heaven, we loose it on earth.**

We loose the four living creatures; We loose revelation;
We loose the fear of the Lord; We loose the Angelic realm.
We loose the Spirit of the Lord!  We loose the Spirit of Glory!

**As it is in heaven, we loose it on earth.**
**The righteous shall rule!  They shall reign!**

www.IntensifiedGloryInstitute.com

## RECOMMENDED RESOURCES:

*CDs*

**Simple Supernatural**
*How to win souls, heal the sick, and minister the baptism of the Holy Spirit*
By Joshua Mills
Distributed by PIP Media Group
P.O. 4037, Palm Springs, CA 92263

*Books*

**Personal Ministry Prayer Manual**
By Joshua & Janet Angela Mills
Published by New Wine International
P.O. Box 4037, Palm Springs, CA 92263

**The Art Of Prayer: A Handbook On How To Pray**
By Kenneth E. Hagin
Published by RHEMA Bible Church
P.O. Box 50126, Tulsa, OK  50126

All resources are available online at:
www.NewWineInternational.org

The Intensified Glory Institute
School of Signs & Wonders

**Lesson #4**
# THE POWER OF PRAISE & WORSHIP

**Course I - Lesson 4**

## THE POWER OF PRAISE & WORSHIP

**Objective:** To understand the power of praise and worship and the role it plays in creating an atmosphere for the glory of God to be expressed through miracles, signs and wonders.

**Overview:** Within this lesson we will search the scriptures and find out what the Word of God says about the power of praise and worship:

- What is the difference between praise and worship?

- How does praise and worship relate to the miraculous?

- Keys for moving into the glory realm through music

- Healing Through Music

- Music And The Frequencies Of Healing

- Biblical Precedent for Supernatural Manifestation Through Music.

**SCRIPTURES FOR MEDITATION:**

☐ Psalm 100:1-5

☐ Psalm 84:4

☐ Psalm 89:1

☐ Revelation 19:5-6

☐ John 4:21-24

The Intensified Glory Institute —————————— NOTES

 **HIDDEN REVELATION**

There is a dimension of music that opens the door to the glory realm – it is the power of praise and worship. Throughout the Word of God we are encouraged to praise the Lord.

## FACTS ABOUT MUSIC

- 1028 scriptural references to music, and over 200 scriptures that tell us to sing!

- God sings (_____), Jesus Christ sings (_____), and the Holy Spirit sings (_____)!

- Music has the ability to break down barriers, open our spirits and soften our hearts. Music has the ability to create an atmosphere. God abides in the praises of His people (Psalm 22:3). Our praise and worship creates an atmosphere for God's glory.

- Sound and music are now being used in traditional fields to enhance learning, treat stress and pain, and bring healing.

- All pain and disease is a result of a lack of vibrational harmony in the body. Under a microscope, cancer cells are "disordered, scattered and diffused," while healthy cells move harmoniously with a sense of balance and ease. The right kind of music can help the body back into harmony. Medical science shows that it has helped dissolve kidney stones, smooth out emotions, relieve painful knees, jaw pain (TMJ syndrome), allergies and more.[1]

- The longest book in the Bible is God's songbook – the Book of Psalms.

---

[1] Dr. Wayne Perry, Heartouch Radio Program

The Intensified Glory Institute ———————————— NOTES

## THE LOCATION OF PRAISE & WORSHIP

When music is performed "horizontally" it can impress people or stir them emotionally, but when music is performed "vertically" it attracts people to the power and presence of God's glory. It carries the ability to lift the musician and those who listen into the heavens. This is what praise and worship is intended to do.

*"Jesus saith unto her, Woman, believe me, the hour cometh, when ye shall neither in this mountain, nor yet at Jerusalem, worship the Father. Ye worship ye know not what: we know what we worship: for salvation is of the Jews. But the hour cometh, and now is, when the true worshippers shall worship the Father in spirit and in truth: for the Father seeketh such to worship him. God is a Spirit: and they that worship him must worship him in spirit and in truth."*
– John 4:21-24

Jesus was speaking with the woman at the well, and He told her that a time was coming when she wouldn't just worship the Father "on the mountain" or "in Jerusalem" but that she would move her worship to another location.

What was the location that Jesus Christ was speaking about?

Jesus said that the true worshipers would worship the Father in a certain location.

_____ and _____

" _____ _____ _____ " is a location – Revelation 1:10-18

## WHAT HAPPENS IN THE SPIRIT?

● Hear the voice of the Lord (vs. 10)

● See Jesus Christ seated on the throne (vs. 13)

● Receive heavenly revelation (vs. 10-18)

www.IntensifiedGloryInstitute.com

The Intensified Glory Institute ——————————— NOTES

_____ is a location - John 16:12-15

## WHAT HAPPENS IN TRUTH?

• You will know things that are "yet to come" (vs. 13)

• You will receive of heavenly blessings (vs. 15)

• The enemy's lies are exposed.  He is not in the truth. (John 8:32)
(ie. No more sickness, disease, infirmity, poverty, discord, etc.)

## WHERE ARE SPIRIT AND TRUTH LOCATED?

These locations are found within the _____ _____.  We move into this location through our praise and worship.

"Come before His presence with singing" – Psalm 100:2

The Lord spoke to Ruth Ward Heflin and gave her an incredible, yet simple, revelation about the heavenly pattern for our praise and worship.

_____… until the spirit of worship comes.

_____… until the glory comes

Then… Stand in the _____

It is a process.  This is the heavenly pattern that God has given to every believer. We move from _____ to _____ to _____.

The Intensified Glory Institute ———————— NOTES

In order to move into this dimension of the glory we must understand the differences between praise and worship:

## WHAT IS PRAISE?

Praise is acknowledging God for
What _____ _____ _____,
What _____ ____ _____ and
What ____ ____ _____ ____ ____!

## WHAT IS WORSHIP?

Worship is acknowledging God for _____ _____ ____.

## WHAT IS THE GLORY?

The glory is a _____ and the glory is a _____. _____ is the glory, and the realm where He dwells is the _____ _____. It is the realm of spirit and truth.

The Intensified Glory Institute —————————— NOTES

# THE DIFFERENCE BETWEEN PRAISE, WORSHIP & GLORY

| IN PRAISE | IN WORSHIP | IN GLORY |
|---|---|---|
| We are loud and exhuberant | We are intimate | We stand in holy stillness |
| We dance and jump | We lift our hands | We connect spirit to spirit |
| We acknowledge what He has done | We acknowledge who He is | We acknowledge His Majestic Greatness |

When we move into the glory through our praise and worship, miracles begin to happen automatically without much effort of our own. We simply see what God is doing and we thank Him for it.

*"And it shall come to pass in that day, that his burden shall be taken away from off thy shoulder, and his yoke from off thy neck, and the yoke shall be destroyed because of the anointing."* - Isaiah 10:27

We use the anointing in praise and worship to bring us into the glory.

All successful miracle ministries have understood this principle:

*Music creates an atmosphere.*

Examples:
- Memories of Childhood
- Romance
- Revival Atmosphere

The Intensified Glory Institute ———————— NOTES

In the Old Testament as the musicians and the singers worshiped together in one accord it created an atmosphere where God was able to reveal Himself through the cloud of His glory!

*"It came even to pass, as the trumpeters and singers were as one, to make one sound to be heard in praising and thanking the LORD; and when they lifted up their voice with the trumpets and cymbals and instruments of musick, and praised the LORD, saying, For he is good; for his mercy endureth for ever: that then the house was filled with a cloud, even the house of the LORD; So that the priests could not stand to minister by reason of the cloud: for the glory of the LORD had filled the house of God."* – 2 Chronicles 5:13-14

*Whenever new songs show up – new miracles show up!*

## HEALING THROUGH MUSIC

1. The Inuit people of eastern Greenland settle their arguments with drums and a song, which they use to discharge their rage toward their enemy. This music brings emotional (inner) healing.

2. In ancient Greece, Rome and Egypt, the priests in the temples sang as they healed the afflicted.

3. In World War II when musicians played for the wounded servicemen, they saw more results than just entertainment from the boredom of hospital life. Depressions lessened, expression increased, and contact with reality improved.[2]

4. Forty patients who had suffered recent heart attacks were exposed to "relaxing music." Results indicated statistically significant reduction in anxiety, respiratory rate, and heart rate, which suggested to researchers that

---

[2] Mitchell L. Gaynor, *The Sounds of Healing* (Broadway, New York, NY 1999) page 78.

the use of music may be an effective way to reduce high levels of anxiety among heart patients.[3]

5. The patients in the coronary care unit who suffered heart attacks had fewer complications when exposed to music for two days than those who were not exposed to it.

6. Drop in stress hormones during medical testing.

7. Lowered blood pressure and heart rate. When listening to a variety of musical styles, both systolic and diastolic blood pressure may decrease by as much as five points per listening session. Heart rate may decrease by four to five beats per minute.

8. At the Addiction Research Center in Stanford, California, subjects listened to various kinds of music. Half of the subjects reported having a feeling of euphoria while listening, leading the researchers to suspect that the joy of music is mediated by the opiate chemicals known as endorphins – the brain's natural painkillers. They concluded that certain kinds of music boost endorphins, which have other health benefits, including a stronger immune system.

---

[3] Dr. Mitchell L. Gaynor, M.D.

# MUSIC AND THE FREQUENCIES OF HEALING

All matter is made up of atoms that are constantly vibrating. Every object has a natural vibratory rate and this is called its resonance. Your body has a resonance. You could even say that your body is a living symphony of music and that you are a song!

All organs, bones, tissues, and every system of the body are in a state of vibration. Each one of these body parts has its own keynote frequency or vibration that is required to function properly.

## KEYNOTE FREQUENCIES

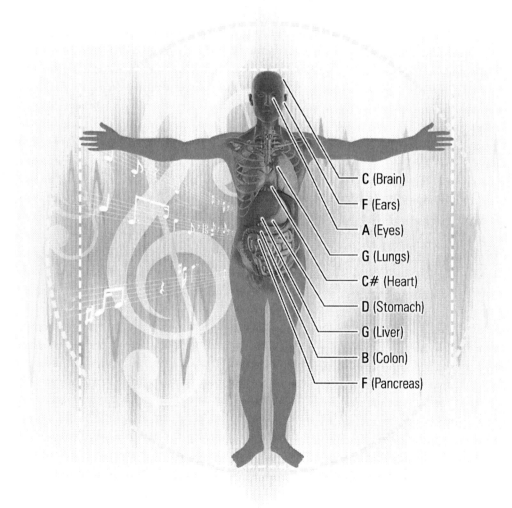

C (Brain)
F (Ears)
A (Eyes)
G (Lungs)
C# (Heart)
D (Stomach)
G (Liver)
B (Colon)
F (Pancreas)

www.IntensifiedGloryInstitute.com

These resonating vibrations found within the body are the very same frequencies found in musical tones, even though the body resonates at a higher level of sound than the natural ear can hear.

Just as the note of "C" appears several times on a piano at varying octaves, the note of "C" appears many times and is the most common frequency within the human body. It is also the keynote frequency of the brain.

When your body is healthy it puts out a vibrational frequency of health. However, when a spirit of sickness (a frequency that is counter to your health) sets itself up in some portion of your body it creates disharmony that is called "dis-ease." The bible says that the power of life and death is in our tongue (Proverbs 18:21) and the Psalms encourage us to sing a NEW song to the Lord!

*"Deep calleth unto deep at the noise of thy waterspouts: all thy waves and thy billows are gone over me. Yet the LORD will command his lovingkindness in the day time, and in the night his song shall be with me, and my prayer unto the God of my life."* – Psalm 42:7-8

In order for our body to be in perfect harmony we must come into alignment with the glory. His song must become our song! The glory is the realm of ease and there is no "dis-ease" in the glory realm.

We were created from, born of and destined for the glory!

God places a special emphasis on praise and worship within the scriptures because we come into His glory through this pattern of living. As we touch the glory of His presence through our song, our body begins to resonate with the heavens and our vibrational frequency is realigned in Jesus Christ.

*"Serve the LORD with gladness: come before his presence with singing."* – Psalm 100:2

Many times we have seen people completely healed by the power of God as they have rested in God's presence during worship.

We have also noticed that people will work better and their days will be more productive when they are in an atmosphere of worship.

When the Lord comes in His glory He begins to do miracles among the masses. Music has always been a major part of any move of God - this is the key to operating in a higher level of miraculous outpouring.

## BIBLICAL PRECEDENT FOR SUPERNATURAL MANIFESTATIONS THROUGH MUSIC

1. _____ **Unction** – 2 Kings 3:15:16

2. **Healing** – Jeremiah 17:14, Luke 17:11-19

3. **Supernatural** _____ – Acts 16:25-26

4. **Manifestation of** _____ – 2 Chronicles 5:13-14

5. **Deliverance from** _____ **spirits** – 1 Samuel 16:14-16, 16:23

6. **Supernatural** _____ – 2 Chronicles 20:22, Joshua 6:20
(Monaco's national orchestra is bigger than its army – they recognize the power of music!)

The Intensified Glory Institute ———————————— NOTES

 **KEYS FOR ACTIVATION**

## CASTING THE NET

*"And it came to pass, that, as the people pressed upon him to hear the word of God, he stood by the lake of Gennesaret,*

*And saw two ships standing by the lake: but the fishermen were gone out of them, and were washing their nets.*

*And he entered into one of the ships, which was Simon's, and prayed him that he would thrust out a little from the land. And he sat down, and taught the people out of the ship.*

*Now when he had left speaking, he said unto Simon, Launch out into the deep, and let down your nets for a draught.*

*And Simon answering said unto him, Master, we have toiled all the night, and have taken nothing: nevertheless at thy word I will let down the net.*

*And when they had this done, they inclosed a great multitude of fishes: and their net brake.*

*And they beckoned unto their partners, which were in the other ship, that they should come and help them. And they came, and filled both the ships, so that they began to sink.*

*When Simon Peter saw it, he fell down at Jesus' knees, saying, Depart from me; for I am a sinful man, O Lord.*

*For he was astonished, and all that were with him, at the draught of the fishes which they had taken."* – Luke 5:1-9

I believe that God wants us to experience a corporate glory together that will bring with it the greatest blessings we've ever known.

It is so important that we enter the glory TOGETHER in times of corporate gatherings. As worshipers it is sometimes easy to forget others behind as we "go ahead" into the glory so easily. We must not lose sight of the bigger picture.

More miracles will happen if more people enter into God's glory!

If the praise and worship doesn't seem to be leading into the glory ("getting anywhere"), cast the net again for a greater result (even if you've already toiled all night!). This is something I learned many years ago as a praise and worship leader in revivals around the world. As you travel to different locations the people will respond differently in praise.

***Always praise until the spirit of worship comes. Don't stop until it does!***

Cast the net where God shows you and you will find the harvest!

# PRAISE WAVES OF GLORY

YOU MAY NEED TO CULTIVATE PRAISE THROUGH CORPORATE DANCE AND PARTICIPATION.

In this photo you can see these **"Praise Waves"** that we form as we corporately usher in the glory of God. People dancing forwards and backwards in a line, as their hands are joined together in unity! This is Psalm 133 in action.

## EXAMPLES OF CULTIVATED CORPORATE PRAISE

- Glory Wheels (people with hands joined together dancing in circles)

- Glory Trains / Jericho March (people joined together as a train marching around the sanctuary)

*Always worship until the glory comes. Don't stop until it does!*

Cast the net until you find the harvest!

## OTHER EXAMPLES FOR "CASTING THE NET" IN WORSHIP

- Many times the Lord will "highlight" a word or phrase. When this phrase is resonating in your spirit, sing this repeatedly as the Lord leads, because there is a special touch of the glory upon it.

- Find the worship song that captures the heart of the people and use this to "cast the net". Many times this is something that is familiar to them. (Examples: *I Exalt Thee, Hallelujah, How Great Is Our God, Glorify Thy Name, etc.*)

www.IntensifiedGloryInstitute.com

The Intensified Glory Institute ———————— NOTES

 **APPLICATIONS FOR HOME**

**1. Make Praise and Worship Your Daily Routine.**

When you become familiar with the power of praise and worship, it will become so simple to enter into the glory on a daily basis. Purpose to start your day by listening to anointed praise and worship music *(Joshua Mills has released several CD's which will start your day in the heavens)*. It is preferable to do this without interruption (as it yields the best results!), but you can also do this by listening as you read your morning devotional, or as you're eating breakfast or even on your drive into work. You will begin to notice a change in your attitude and work efficiency when you start your day this way!

**2. Take a "SpiritSpa" - Soak with Worship Music**

The bible says that "times of refreshing come in the presence of the Lord". Spend time in the atmosphere of God's presence through taking a daily (or weekly) SpiritSpa. Just lie down in a comfortable location and turn on some peaceful worship music. It is more ideal to listen to praise and worship through a sound system with speakers (as opposed to headphones) as the cells of your body themselves will "listen" and begin to respond positively. When the music stops, just bask in the silence and begin to listen for the still small voice of the Lord. *(Joshua Mills' "SpiritSpa" instrumental piano CD is available for ordering online or digital download at: www.NewWineInternational.org)*

**3. Listen Actively, Not Passively**

Allow the praise and worship to reach your inmost feelings, and begin to respond to it. When God begins speaking to your heart through music, begin responding back to Him in a song or some other way. Everyone has a different manner of expression. You may experience visions, thoughts, movement, an intense emotion, physical vibrations, a sense of rest/sleep, or nothing at all. Simply be free! You will find that your response will increase as you return it unto Him. It is also through your response that the emotional/cellular memory may be released into God's presence!

## 4. Watch For Miracles!

As you corporately participate in praise and worship during church and conference meetings, begin to watch for the miracles. Become aware of changes in your physical body – the healing miracles that God is working inside of you! Become aware of the change in the corporate atmosphere. Begin looking for signs and wonders all around you because they manifest through the power of praise and worship!

## RECOMMENDED RESOURCES:

*CDs*

**Praise Changes The Atmosphere**
By Joshua Mills
Released by PIP Media Group
P.O. Box 4037, Palm Springs, CA 92263

**SpiritSpa: Intrumental Piano**
By Joshua Mills
Released by PIP Media Group
P.O. Box 4037, Palm Springs, CA 92263

**Holy Invasion – Live from Paramount Pictures Studios**
By Joshua & Janet Angela Mills and friends
Released by PIP Media Group
P.O. Box 4037, Palm Springs, CA 92263

*Books*

**Into His Presence: Praise & Worship Manual**
By Joshua Mills
Published by New Wine International
P.O. Box 4037, Palm Springs, CA 92263

**Glory: Experiencing The Atmosphere Of Heaven**
By Ruth Ward Heflin
Published by McDougal Publishing
P.O. Box 3595, Hagerstown, MD 21742

All resources are available online at:
www.NewWineInternational.org

The Intensified Glory Institute ———————————— NOTES

# Course I - Lesson 4

## THE POWER OF PRAISE & WORSHIP

### SCRIPTURE REFERENCES I

#### PRAISE

| | | | | | |
|---|---|---|---|---|---|
| Gen 29:35 | Ps 21:13 | Ps 56:4 | Ps 102:18 | Ps 117:2 | Jer 13:11 |
| Deut 10:21 | Ps 22:22 | Ps 56:10 | Ps 102:21 | Ps 118:19 | Jer 17:14 |
| Judg 5:2 | Ps 22:23 | Ps 57:7 | Ps 104:33 | Ps 118:21 | Jer 17:26 |
| Judg 5:3 | Ps 22:25 | Ps 57:9 | Ps 104:35 | Ps 118:28 | Jer 20:13 |
| 1 Chr 16:4 | Ps 22:26 | Ps 61:8 | Ps 105:45 | Ps 119:7 | Jer 31:7 |
| 1 Chr 16:35 | Ps 28:7 | Ps 63:3 | Ps 106:1 | Ps 119:164 | Jer 33:9 |
| 1 Chr 23:5 | Ps 30:9 | Ps 63:5 | Ps 106:2 | Ps 119:171 | Jer 33:11 |
| 1 Chr 23:30 | Ps 30:12 | Ps 65:1 | Ps 106:12 | Ps 119:175 | Dan 2:23 |
| 1 Chr 25:3 | Ps 33:1 | Ps 66:2 | Ps 106:47 | Ps 135:1-2 | Dan 4:37 |
| 1 Chr 29:13 | Ps 33:2 | Ps 66:8 | Ps 106:48 | Ps 135:21 | Joel 2:26 |
| 2 Chr 7:6 | Ps 34:1 | Ps 67:3 | Ps 107:8 | Ps 138:1 | Hab 3:3 |
| 2 Chr 8:14 | Ps 35:18 | Ps 67:5 | Ps 107:15 | Ps 149:1 | Matt 21:16 |
| 2 Chr 20:19 | Ps 35:28 | Ps 69:30 | Ps 107:21 | Ps 149:3 | Luke 18:43 |
| 2 Chr 20:21 | Ps 40:3 | Ps 69:34 | Ps 107:31 | Ps 149:9 | Luke 19:37 |
| 2 Chr 20:22 | Ps 42:4 | Ps 71:6 | Ps 107:32 | Ps 150:1 | John 9:24 |
| 2 Chr 29:30 | Ps 42:5 | Ps 71:8 | Ps 108:1 | Ps 150:2 | Rom 2:29 |
| 2 Chr 31:2 | Ps 42:11 | Ps 71:14 | Ps 108:3 | Ps 150:6 | Rom 15:11 |
| Ezra 3:10 | Ps 43:4 | Ps 71:22 | Ps 109:1 | Prov 31:31 | 1 Cor 4:5 |
| Neh 9:5 | Ps 43:5 | Ps 74:21 | Ps 109:30 | Isa 21:1 | Eph 1:6 |
| Neh 12:24 | Ps 44:8 | Ps 76:10 | Ps 111:1 | Isa 21:4 | Eph 1:12 |
| Neh 12:46 | Ps 45:17 | Ps 79:13 | Ps 111:10 | Isa 25:1 | Eph 1:14 |
| Ps 7:17 | Ps 48:10 | Ps 86:12 | Ps 112:1 | Isa 38:18-19 | Phil 1:11 |
| Ps 9:1 | Ps 49:18 | Ps 88:10 | Ps 113:1 | Isa 42:8-12 | Phil 4:8 |
| Ps 9:2 | Ps 50:23 | Ps 89:5 | Ps 113:9 | Isa 43:21 | Heb 2:12 |
| Ps 9:14 | Ps 51:15 | Ps 98:4 | Ps 115:17 | Isa 60:18 | Heb 13:15 |
| | Ps 52:9 | Ps 99:3 | Ps 115:18 | Isa 61:11 | 1 Pet 1:7 |
| | Ps 54:6 | Ps 100:4 | Ps 116:19 | Isa 62:7 | 1 Pet 4:11 |
| | | | Ps 117:1 | Isa 62:9 | Rev 19:5 |

105

## Course I - Lesson 4

## THE POWER OF PRAISE & WORSHIP

| SCRIPTURE REFERENCES II | | |
|---|---|---|
| **WORSHIP** | | |
| Gen 22:5 | Ps 138:2 | John 4:22 |
| Exod 24:1 | Isa 27:13 | John 4:23 |
| Exod 34:14 | Isa 36:7 | John 4:24 |
| Deut 26:10 | Isa 49:7 | Acts 7:42 |
| 1 Sam 1:3 | Isa 66:23 | Acts 8:27 |
| 1 Sam 15:25 | Jer 7:2 | Acts 18:13 |
| 1 Sam 15:30 | Jer 26:2 | Acts 24:11 |
| 2 Kings 17:36 | Ezek 46:2 | Acts 24:14 |
| 2 Kings 18:22 | Ezek 46:3 | 1 Cor 14:25 |
| 1 Chr 16:29 | Ezek 46:9 | Phil 3:3 |
| Ps 5:7 | Dan 3:28 | Col 2:23 |
| Ps 22:27 | Zeph 1:5 | Heb 1:16 |
| Ps 22:29 | Zeph 2:11 | Rev 3:9 |
| Ps 29:2 | Zeph 14:16 | Rev 4:10 |
| Ps 45:11 | Zeph 14:17 | Rev 11:1 |
| Ps 66:4 | Matt 2:2 | Rev 13:8 |
| Ps 81:9 | Matt 2:8 | Rev 14:7 |
| Ps 86:9 | Matt 4:10 | Rev 15:4 |
| Ps 95:6 | Matt 15:9 | Rev 19:10 |
| Ps 96:9 | Mark 7:7 | |
| Ps 97:7 | Luke 4:8 | |
| Ps 99:5 | Luke 14:10 | |
| Ps 99:9 | John 4:20 | |
| Ps 132:7 | John 4:21 | |

# The Intensified Glory Institute
# School of Signs & Wonders

## Lesson #5
## ACTIVATING ANGELS

## Course I - Lesson 5

## ACTIVATING ANGELS

**Objective:** To understand and become aware of the purpose of Angels and God's intended purpose for the ministry of the Angelic realm in the life of every believer.

**Overview:** Within this lesson we will search the scriptures and find out what the Word of God says about the supernatural Angelic realm and we will learn how we can begin activating Angels:

- The Purpose of Angels

- The Different Types of Heavenly Beings

- Facts About Angels

- The Ministry Of Angels

- The Appearance Of Angels

- Reactions To The Angelic Realm

- How To Activate The Angelic Realm In Your Life

**SCRIPTURES FOR MEDITATION:**

☐ Psalm 91:11-12

☐ Matthew 6:33

☐ Hebrews 1

The Intensified Glory Institute ———————— NOTES

## 🔒 HIDDEN REVELATION

Jesus Christ is _____ _____ ____ _____, but God created the Angelic realm to play an _____ _____ in God's work with humanity.

Angels are mentioned at least ____ times in the Old Testament and ____ times in the New Testament.

If the Lord has given us this much information in His Word about this realm, I believe that God wants us to understand the role that Angels play in our daily lives.

The word *"Angel"* actually comes from the Greek word *"aggelos"* which means _____. The Hebrew word has the same meaning as well.

## ANGELS

There are many other names used in the Holy Bible to refer to Angels:

- Heavenly Hosts
- Sons of God
- Holy Ones
- Watchers
- Armies Of Heaven
- Heavenly Beings

## THE PURPOSE OF ANGELS

a. ___ _____ ____ _____ (Deut. 32:43, Psalm 148:2, Isaiah 6:1-3)

b. ___ ____ __ ___ _____ (Revelation 12:7-9)

c. ____ _____ ____ _____ (Hebrews 1:14)

The Intensified Glory Institute ——————————— NOTES

# DIFFERENT TYPES OF HEAVENLY BEINGS

**1. Seraphim**

The name Seraphim means "the burning ones." _____ _____ emanates from them so that nothing can look upon them. They serve as the _____ of God's throne and continuously sing praise to the Lord. Psalm 104:4, Isaiah 6:1-7.

**2. Cherubim**

Cherubim are an order of Angels with wings that guard the holiness of God's light and glory. They _____ the throne of God. Genesis 3:24, Ezekiel 28:14-16, 1 Kings 6:23-28.

**3. Thrones (Elders)**

The Thrones and Elders are intensely _____ Angels that are living symbols of God's _____ and _____. Colossians 1:16, Revelation 11:16.

**4. Dominions (Heavenly Lights)**

These are the Angels who preside _____ _____. They are physically characterized from other Angels as wielding _____ of _____. Genesis 1:1-5, James 1:17, Colossians 1:16.

**5. Archangels (Chief Angel)**

These are the highest ranking Angels. _____ and _____ are considered Archangels. Dan 10:11-21, 1 Thessalonians 4:16, Jude 1:9.

**6. The Living Creatures**

They have _____ _____: one of each a man, an ox, a lion and an eagle. They are covered with _____ and _____. Ezekiel 10, Revelation 4:6-5:14.

**7. Spirit Animals**

These animals in heaven are shaped like the fleshly ones we have on earth. Romans 1:20, 2 Corinthians 12:1-4, Revelation 19:11-21.

**8. Spirit Horses and Angelic Chariot Drivers**

These Spirit Horses sometimes appear as a _____ or in various colors as red, brown and white. 2 Kings 2:11-12, 2 Kings 6:13-17, Zechariah 1:8-11.

**9. Common Angels**

They are heavenly spirit beings with _____ _____ _____ including hands, feet, eyes, heads, hair, voices, mouths, faces, and other parts which men have (Genesis 18:2-8, 19:1-22, Judges 13:6). They have _____ _____ with _____ (Luke 15:1-10), compassions (Genesis 6:1-4), appetites (Genesis 18:8, 19:3), desires (1 Peter 1:12) and other soul passions and feelings. They are _____ _____ with intelligence and wisdom (2 Samuel 14:20, 19:27, Matthew 24:36), meekness (2 Peter 2:11), modesty (1 Corinthians 11:10), holiness (Mark 8:38), obedience (Psalm 103:20), knowledge (Mark 13:32), willpower (Isaiah 14:12-14), ability to speak languages (1 Corinthians 13:1) and other spirit abilities.

## FACTS ABOUT ANGELS

1. They are not to be _____ – Colossians 2:18, Revelation 19:10, 22:9

2. They are without sex, but may appear in either _____ or _____ form. Angels are always referred to in the masculine gender, except for one scriptural reference in Zechariah.  Matthew 22:30, Genesis 19:10-12, Zechariah 5:9

3. They are _____ and have _____ _____, but they are not omnipotent – Luke 20:36

4. They do not need _____ – Revelation 4:8

5. They are _____ – Psalm 103:20, Matthew 6:10

6. They can travel at inconceivable _____ – Ezekiel 1, Revelation 8:13

7. They can ascend and descend – John 1:51

8. They are commonly described in _____ _____ – Psalm 68:17, Matthew 26:53, Hebrews 12:22

9. According to the bible, Angels are not those who have died in Christ. _____ _____ become part of the "Great Cloud of Witness" not another class of angels.

10. Jesus Christ received _____ and _____ through the ministry of Angels – Luke 22:43

*"Father, if you are willing, take this cup from me; yet not my will, but yours be done." An angel from heaven appeared to him and strengthened him. And being in anguish, he prayed more earnestly, and his sweat was like drops of blood falling to the ground." – Luke 22:42-44*

# THE MINISTRY OF ANGELS

*"Are not the angels all ministering spirits (servants) sent out in the service [of God for the assistance] of those who are to inherit salvation?"* – Hebrews 1:14

1. **Guardians of** _____ – Psalm 34:7, Psalm 91:11-12, Matthew 18:10, Luke 4:10, Acts 12:7-10

2. **Minister to** _____ – Daniel 6:22, Acts 10

3. **Rule** _____ – Daniel 10:13-21, 12:1

4. **Minister** _____ – Psalm 16:11, Luke 2:10, Luke 15:10

5. **Deliver** _____ – Genesis 24:40, 1 Kings 19:5-7

6. _____ _____ – John 5:2-4, Luke 1:11

7. **Help Gather the** _____ – Acts 10:3, Mark 13:27

8. **Direct** _____ – Acts 8:26

9. **Give** _____ – Exodus 23:20-23, 2 Kings 1:3, 1:15, Daniel 8:19, 9:21-23, Luke 1, Acts 27:21-25

10. _____ _____ – 2 Thessalonians 1:7-10, Revelation 12:7-9

11. **Guard The Abyss** – Revelation 9:1, 20:1-3

12. **Bring** _____ **To** _____ – Daniel 9:21-28

13. _____ **People During Trials** – Matthew 4:11

14. **Regather** _____ – Matthew 24:31

15. **Appear In** _____ – Matthew 1:20-24

16. **Punish God's** _____ – Acts 12:23, 2 Samuel 24:16

17. _____ _____ _____ – Revelation 8:2, 14:15-19

*"The angel of the Lord encampeth round about*
*them that fear him, and delivereth them."*
– Psalm 34:7

www.IntensifiedGloryInstitute.com

The Intensified Glory Institute ———————————— NOTES

## THE APPEARANCE OF ANGELS

1. **Invisible** – Colossians 1:16, 2 Kings 6:17

2. **Guardian Angels** look like us! – Acts 12:6-17

3. **Other People** (Male or Female) – Hebrews 13:2, Luke 24:4

4. **Shafts of light / Orbs** – James 1:17, Luke 2:9

5. **Fire / Lightning** – Exodus 3:2, Daniel 10:5-6, Hebrews 1:7

6. **Wind** – Hebrews 1:7

7. **Animals** – Ezekiel 10, Zechariah 1:8-11

8. **Dreams / Visions** – Genesis 28:11-17

9. **Aura of Rainbow Light** – Revelation 10:1

## REACTIONS TO THE ANGELIC REALM IN SCRIPTURE

1. _____ – Luke 1:12, Luke 2:13-14

2. Fear Of The Lord / _____ – Luke 1:26-28

3. _____ _____ – John 20:11-13, Acts 1:9-11

The Intensified Glory Institute ———————— NOTES

## KEYS FOR ACTIVATION

*"Hasten and come, all you nations round about, and assemble yourselves; there You, O Lord, will bring down Your mighty ones (Your warriors)."* – Joel 3:11

In the above scripture we see that the Prophet Joel called upon the Lord to activate the Angelic realm in his life.

- Abraham released an Angel – Genesis 24:1,4-7, 40

- Elisha released the Angels – 2 Kings 6:8-17

It is possible for us to do the same – releasing the Angels of God in our lives today.

We find some great keys for activation in the book of Psalms and in the story of Cornelius in Acts 10:1-4.

*"Bless (affectionately, gratefully praise) the Lord, <u>you His angels</u>, you mighty ones who do His commandments, <u>hearkening to the voice of His word.</u>  Bless (affectionately, gratefully praise) the Lord, all you His hosts, <u>you His ministers who do His pleasure.</u>"* – Psalm 103:20-21

*"Now [living] at Caesarea there was a man whose name was Cornelius, a centurion (captain) of what was known as the Italian Regiment.  A devout man who venerated God and treated Him with reverential obedience, as did all his household; and <u>he gave much alms</u> to the people and <u>prayed continually to God.</u> About the ninth hour (about 3:00 p.m.) of the day he saw clearly in a vision an angel of God entering and saying to him, Cornelius.  And he, gazing intently at him, became frightened and said, What is it, Lord?  And the angel said to him, <u>Your prayers and your [generous] gifts</u> to the poor <u>have come up [as a sacrifice] to God</u> and have been remembered by Him."*
– Acts 10:1-4

The Intensified Glory Institute —————————————— NOTES

## THE S.I.T. PRINCIPLE

Here are three primary keys to activating the Angelic realm in your life. Find some quiet time with the Lord and begin using these keys as a guideline.

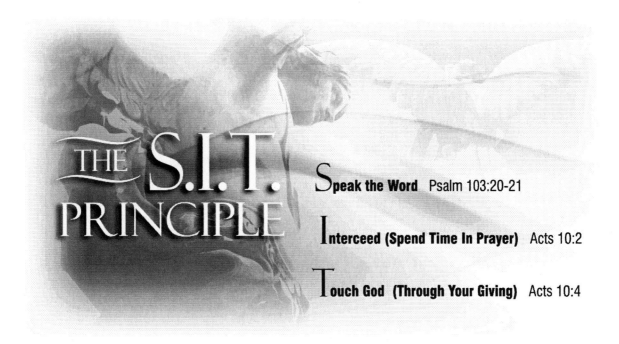

**S**peak the Word   Psalm 103:20-21

**I**nterceed (Spend Time In Prayer)   Acts 10:2

**T**ouch God   (Through Your Giving)   Acts 10:4

*"Be still, and know that I am God;*
*I will be exalted among the nations,*
*I will be exalted in the earth."*
– Psalm 46:10 (NIV)

The Intensified Glory Institute —————————————— NOTES

## APPLICATIONS FOR HOME

1. **Become more familiar with your surroundings**.
   Begin to pay attention to things like flashes of light, heavenly sounds, unusual appearances of rainbows, light breezes and the small changes in atmospheric conditions around you. These could be the presence of God's ministering Angels in your life. When you notice these things, prayerfully ask the Lord what He is doing and revealing to you.

2. **Take notice of your photographs.**
   Many people are beginning to notice the Angelic realm appearing in their digital photography as "heavenly lights." Become aware of the difference between water moisture/dust in the air and the genuine supernatural orbs. When you see Angels appearing in your photos, pray and ask the Lord what He is saying through it.

3. **Read and Meditate on the Word.**
   You can use the time before bed to meditate upon God's word and read biblical accounts of Angelic visitation. At night you are the most relaxed and God is able to use this time to speak to you and show you things through dreams and visions. Other recommended reading is *"Angels On Assignment"* written by Pastor Roland Buck.

4. **Remember to S.I.T.**
   Speak the Word, Intercede and Touch God with Your Giving!
   (These are the keys provided above).

The Intensified Glory Institute ——————————— NOTES

## Course I – Lesson 5

## ACTIVATING ANGELS

### SCRIPTURE REFERENCES

| ANGEL | | ANGELS | |
|---|---|---|---|
| Gen. 16:7-11, 21:17 22:11, 24:40, 48:16 Exodus 3:2, 23:20 Num. 20:16, 22:22 Ecclesiastes 5:6 John 5:4, 12:29 Acts 5:19, 6:15, 7:30 | 2 Corinthians 11:14 Galatians 1:8, 4:14 Revelation 1:1, 2:1, 2:8, 2:12, 2:18, 3:1, 3:7, 3:14, 5:2, 7:2, 8:3, 8:7, 10:1, 11:15, 14:6, 16:5, 22:16 | Genesis 19:1, 19:15, 28:12, 32:1 Job 4:18 Psalm 8:5, 68:17, 78:25, 78:49, 91:11 103:20, 104:4, 148:2, Jude 1:6 | Matthew 4:6, 4:11, 13:39, 13:41, 13:49, 16:27, 18:10, 22:30, Mark 1:13, 8:38, 12:25, 13:27, 13:32 Luke 2:15, 4:10, 9:26 Acts 7:53 |

| HOLY ONES | WATCHER | SONS OF GOD |
|---|---|---|
| Job 5:1, 15:15 Psalm 89:7 Daniel 4:13, 17, 23 Daniel 8:13 Jude 14 Acts 7:53 Galatians 3:19 Hebrews 2:2 | (Full of eyes, also known as: The Living Creatures)<br><br>Daniel 4:13 Ezekiel 1:18 Revelation 4:6, 8 | Colossians 1:16 John 1:3 Hebrews 1:2,10 Job 1:6 Job 2:1 Job 38:7 |

| THE LORD OF "HOSTS" | HEAVENLY HOST |
|---|---|
| Exodus 12:41 1 Samuel 1:3, 1:11, 4:4, 15:2, 17:45 2 Samuel 5:10, 6:2, 6:18, 7:8, 7:26, 7:27 1 Kings 18:15, 19:10, 10:14, 2 Kings 3:14, 19:31 1 Chronicles 11:9, 17:7, 17:24 Psalms 24:10, 46:7, 46:11, 48:8, 59:5, 103:21 Isaiah 1:9, 1:24, 2:12, 3:3, 3:15, 5:7, 5:9 Jeremiah 2:19, 5:14, 6:6, 6:9, 7:3, 7:21 Hosea 12:5, Amos 3:13, 4:13, 5:14-16 Zephaniah 2:9, 2:10, Haggai 1:2, 2:6-9 Zechariah 1:3, 1:4, 1:6, 1:12, 1:14, 1:16-17 Malachi 1:4, 1:6, 1:8-11, 2:2, 2:4, 2:7, 2:12 | Genesis 2:1, 32:2 Joshua 5:13-15 1 Kings 22:19 2 Kings 17:6, 21:3, 21:4, 21:5 2 Chronicles 14:13, 18:18, 33:3, 33:5 Nehemiah 9:6 Isaiah 34:4 Jeremiah 8:2, 19:13, 33:22 Daniel 8:10 1 Samuel 17:45 Psalm 86:6,8 Luke 3:13 Acts 7:42 |

### 127

## RECOMMENDED RESOURCES:

*CDs*

**Ministering with Angels:** *How To Activate the Angelic Realm in Your Life*
By Joshua Mills
Released by PIP Media Group
P.O. Box 4037, Palm Springs, CA 92263

*Books*

**Angels On Assignment**
By Roland Buck
Published by Whitaker House
1030 Hunt Valley Circle, New Kensington, PA  15068

**The Angel Book**
By Charles & Frances Hunter
Published by Whitaker House
1030 Hunt Valley Circle, New Kensington, PA  15068

**Angels:** *Knowing Their Purpose, Releasing Their Power*
By Charles Capps
Published by Harrison House
P.O. Box 35035, Tulsa, OK  74153

All resources are available online at:
www.NewWineInternational.org

# The Intensified Glory Institute
# School of Signs & Wonders

## Lesson #6
## EXPLORING REALMS OF HEAVENLY GLORY

## Course I - Lesson 6

## EXPLORING REALMS OF HEAVENLY GLORY

**Objective:** To understand and begin to explore the realms of heaven within the context of scripture and modern day experiences.

**Overview:** Within this lesson we will search the scriptures and find out what the Word of God says about the realms of Heavenly Glory:

- Where is Heaven?

- What does Heaven look like?

- Facts About Heaven

- Scriptural Encounters of Heavenly Experience

- Purpose For Heavenly Encounters

**SCRIPTURES FOR MEDITATION:**

☐ Revelation 22:1-5

☐ 2 Corinthians 3:17-18

☐ Ephesians 2:2-7

131

The Intensified Glory Institute ——————— NOTES

# HIDDEN REVELATION

God has given us an eternal promise for our walk of faith. In the following scripture passage we read about the sacrifices that our forefathers made in order to believe God and live a life of faith.

*"By faith Abraham, when he was called to go out into a place which he should after receive for an inheritance, obeyed; and he went out, not knowing whither he went. By faith he sojourned in the land of promise, as in a strange country, dwelling in tabernacles with Isaac and Jacob, the heirs with him of the same promise: For he looked for a city which hath foundations, whose builder and maker is God. Through faith also Sara herself received strength to conceive seed, and was delivered of a child when she was past age, because she judged him faithful who had promised. Therefore sprang there even of one, and him as good as dead, so many as the stars of the sky in multitude, and as the sand which is by the sea shore innumerable. These all died in faith, not having received the promises, but having seen them afar off, and were persuaded of them, and embraced them, and confessed that they were strangers and pilgrims on the earth. For they that say such things declare plainly that they seek a country. And truly, if they had been mindful of that country from whence they came out, they might have had opportunity to have returned. But now they desire a better country, that is, an heavenly: wherefore God is not ashamed to be called their God: for he hath prepared for them a city."* – Hebrews 11:8-16

Our faith has a purpose – and that eternal purpose is the reward of heaven! As we walk by faith, we are rewarded with the privileged opportunity to explore the realms of heavenly glory.

The Intensified Glory Institute ——————————— NOTES

## THE THREE REALMS OF HEAVEN

The word Heaven is used over _____ times in the Bible.

As we begin to explore realms of heavenly glory we must understand that there are three distinct "heavens" that exist. The bible speaks about all three, and we must be able to differentiate these heavens as we desire to explore the heavenly realm where God abides.

1. **The _____ Heaven** – the _____ and _____ above us.

This heaven is the domain in which we live.

*"In the beginning God created the heaven and the earth."*
– Genesis 1:1

*"Where were you when I laid the earth's foundation? Tell me, if you understand. Who marked off its dimensions? Surely you know! Who stretched a measuring line across it? On what were its footings set, or who laid its cornerstone while the morning stars sang together and all the angels shouted for joy?"* – Job 38:4-7 (NIV)

*"And I saw a new heaven and a new earth: for the first heaven and the first earth were passed away…"* – Revelation 21:1

2. **The _____ Heaven** – the cosmic heaven of _____ _____.

This heaven is the domain for principalities and rulers of darkness.

*"In that day the LORD will punish the powers in the heavens above and the kings on the earth below."* – Isaiah 24:21 (NIV)

*"For we wrestle not against flesh and blood, but against principalities, against powers, against the rulers of the darkness of this world, against spiritual wickedness in high places."* – Ephesians 6:12

www.IntensifiedGloryInstitute.com

The Intensified Glory Institute ———————————— NOTES

*"For our struggle is not against flesh and blood, but against the rulers, against the authorities, against the powers of this dark world and against the spiritual forces of evil in the heavenly realms."*
– Ephesians 6:12 (NIV)

3. **The _____ Heaven** – above and beyond the realm of outer space. This heaven is the Abode of God or what is referred to as _____

*"I must go on boasting. Although there is nothing to be gained, I will go on to visions and revelations from the Lord.  I know a man in Christ who fourteen years ago was caught up to the third heaven. Whether it was in the body or out of the body I do not know—God knows.  And I know that this man—whether in the body or apart from the body I do not know, but God knows— was caught up to paradise. He heard inexpressible things, things that man is not permitted to tell. I will boast about a man like that, but I will not boast about myself, except about my weaknesses.  Even if I should choose to boast, I would not be a fool, because I would be speaking the truth. But I refrain, so no one will think more of me than is warranted by what I do or say."* – 2 Corinthians 12:1-6 (NIV)

*"He that hath an ear, let him hear what the Spirit saith unto the churches; To him that overcometh will I give to eat of the tree of life, which is in the midst of the paradise of God."* – Revelation 2:7

*"The highest heavens belong to the LORD, but the earth he has given to man."* – Psalm 115:16 (NIV)

When Jesus Christ was on the earth He was teaching his disciples how to pray and he said a very specific prayer.  In Matthew 6:9, Jesus prayed:

*"Thy kingdom come, thy will be done on earth as it is in heaven."*

**On earth as it is in heaven**… those were the words that Jesus spoke.  Many Christians don't have any understanding of what "it is like" in heaven.  For most Christians, heaven is a place far away that will be reached one day after death.  We need to search the scriptures to find out what the bible says about the

137

The Intensified Glory Institute ———————————— NOTES

Third Heaven, because Jesus prayed that we would experience these realms of glory while we are still here on the earth!

*What kind of images do you see in your mind, when you think of heaven coming to earth?*

## FACTS ABOUT THE THIRD HEAVEN

1. **Heaven Is** _____

*"Surely goodness and mercy shall follow me all the days of my life: and I will dwell in the house of the LORD forever."* – Psalm 23:6

*"And these shall go away into everlasting punishment: but the righteous into life eternal."* – Matthew 25:46

*"And I give unto them eternal life; and they shall never perish..."* – John 10:28

*"...an inheritance incorruptible, and undefiled, and that fadeth not away, reserved in heaven for you."* – 1 Peter 1:4

*"...an entrance shall be ministered unto you abundantly into the everlasting kingdom of our Lord and Saviour Jesus Christ."* – 2 Peter 1:11

*"And there shall be no night there; and they need no candle, neither light of the sun; for the Lord God giveth them light: and they shall reign forever and ever."* – Revelation 22:5

2. **Heaven Is God's** _____ _____

*"Look down from thy holy habitation, from heaven, and bless thy people Israel..."* – Deuteronomy 26:15

*"...hear thou in heaven thy dwelling place..."* – 1 Kings 8:30

*"For he hath looked down from the height of his sanctuary; from heaven did the LORD behold the earth."* – Psalm 102:19

*"Unto thee lift I up mine eyes, O thou that dwellest in the heavens."* – Psalm 123:1

*"For thus saith the high and lofty One that inhabiteth eternity, whose name is Holy; I dwell in the high and holy place…"* – Isaiah 57:15

*"Now of the things which we have spoken this is the sum: We have such an high priest, who is set on the right hand of the throne of the Majesty in the heavens."* – Hebrews 8:1

3.  **Only the _____ Can Enter Into Heaven**

*"Envyings, murders, drunkenness, revellings, and such like: of the which I tell you before, as I have also told you in time past, that they which do such things shall not inherit the kingdom of God."* – Galatians 5:21

*"For this ye know, that no whoremonger, nor unclean person, nor covetous man, who is an idolater, hath any inheritance in the kingdom of Christ and of God."* – Ephesians 5:5

God is very careful about who He invites into His home. Our hearts and motives must be pure.

4.  **People Of All _____ And Every _____ Will Be Represented**

*"And they sung a new song, saying, Thou art worthy to take the book, and to open the seals thereof: for thou wast slain, and hast redeemed us to God by thy blood out of every kindred, and tongue, and people, and nation…"* – Revelation 5:9

*"After this I beheld, and, lo, a great multitude, which no man could number, of all nations, and kindreds, and people, and tongues, stood before the throne, and before the Lamb, clothed with white robes, and palms in their hands."*
– Revelation 7:9

## WHAT IS HEAVEN LIKE?

### 1. Heaven Is Beautiful

*"And I John saw the holy city, new Jerusalem, coming down from God out of heaven, prepared as a bride adorned for her husband."* – Revelation 21:2

Revelation 21:11, 18-19, 21

### 2. There Is Continual Praise & Worship

Nehemiah 9:6
Job 38:7
Psalm 103:20-21
Psalm 148:2,4
Isaiah 6:3
Ezekiel 3:12
Luke 2:13-14
Luke 15:10

*The Book of Revelation is Heaven's Songbook!*

Revelation 1:6          Revelation 4:8-11
Revelation 5:9-14       Revelation 7:9-12
Revelation 11:16-17     Revelation 14:2-3
Revelation 15:3-4       Revelation 19:1-7
Revelation 22:3

141

### 3. Heaven Is A Place Of Great Joy!

Psalm 16:11
Psalm 17:15
Isaiah 33:17
Isaiah 49:9-10
Matthew 5:8
Luke 15:7,10
1 Thessalonians 4:17
Hebrews 12:22-23

### 4. There is Laughter in Heaven

Psalm 2:4

### 5. No Sickness or Pain

Revelation 21:4

### 6. No Sorrow, Crying or Mourning

Revelation 7:17
Revelation 21:4

### 7. No Violence or Wars

Job 3:17
2 Thessalonians 1:7

### 8. No More Death

Luke 20:36
Revelation 21:4

9. **No More Hunger Or Thirst**

Revelation 7:16-17

## WORDS THAT DESCRIBE HEAVEN

- The Father's House – John 14:2, Psalm 23:6

- A Heavenly Country / City – Hebrews 11:10,16, Hebrews 13:14

- The Kingdom Of God – Matthew 13:43, Luke 12:32, Ephesians 5:5

- Paradise – Luke 23:43, 2 Corinthians 12:2-4, Revelation 2:7

- The Mountain Of The Lord – Hebrews 12:22, Revelation 14:1-3

- A Great Feast (Celebration) – Matthew 8:11, Luke 22:30

## WHERE IS HEAVEN?

Some scriptures relate Heaven as being a "place up in the sky":

*"And it came to pass, as they still went on, and talked, that, behold, there appeared a chariot of fire, and horses of fire, and parted them both asunder; and Elijah went up by a whirlwind into heaven."* - 2 Kings 2:11

*"But he, being full of the Holy Ghost, looked up stedfastly into heaven, and saw the glory of God, and Jesus standing on the right hand of God, And said, Behold, I see the heavens opened, and the Son of man standing on the right hand of God."* – Acts 7:55-56

Other scriptures relate Heaven as being within us:

- Matthew 3:2, Matthew 4:17, Mark 1:15, Luke 17:20-21

We must not think that God has two homes – a residential home and a vacation condo! When God comes to us He brings Heaven with Him, just like the rain! He is the Glory!

- Revelation 21:3
- Isaiah 57:13 – Possessing the Holy Mountain
- Deuteronomy 1:21
- Psalm 91:1-2

## HEAVENLY ENCOUNTERS IN THE BIBLE

- Prophet Isaiah – Isaiah 6:1-4

- Paul – 2 Corinthians 12:1-2,4

- John The Revelator – Revelation 4:1-2

- Ezekiel – Ezekiel 1, 3:12-14

- Great Cloud Of Witnesses – Hebrews 12:1-2

## THE PURPOSE OF EXPLORING THE HEAVENLY REALM

### Revelation

- *"I will show you things which must take place"* (Revelation 4)

- *"I saw the Lord sitting on a throne"* (Isaiah 6:1-4)

- *"...heard inexpressible words..."* (2 Corinthians 12:1-2)

- Ezekiel saw and He became!

## Jesus Was Constantly Receiving Revelation From Heaven

- John 5:19-20

## God Desires To Give Us Revelation For:

- Creative Soul-winning and Salvations

- Miracles

- Harvest (Spiritual & Physical)

*Remember that revelation brings manifestation!*

NOTES

# KEYS FOR ACTIVATION

## 4 KEYS FOR EXPLORING REALMS OF HEAVENLY GLORY

*"But because of his great love for us, God, who is rich in mercy, made us alive with Christ even when we were dead in transgressions—it is by grace you have been saved. And God raised us up with Christ and seated us with him in the heavenly realms in Christ Jesus, in order that in the coming ages he might show the incomparable riches of his grace, expressed in his kindness to us in Christ Jesus."* – Ephesians 2:4-7

### 1. Pure Motives & Pure Heart

I want you to see in the scriptures that seeing, perceiving and receiving revelation are all connected to issues of the heart:

- Matthew 13:14-15

- Matthew 5:8

- Psalm 24:3-4

- James 4:8

What is your motive for exploring the realms of heaven? Do you want to see Him or do you want to be seen?

### 2. Set Your Mind On Heavenly Things

- James 4:8

- Colossians 3:2

- Philippians 4:8

- Ezekiel 1, 3:12-14

### 3. Expectation For Invitation

*"After this I looked, and there before me was a door standing open in heaven. And the voice I had first heard speaking to me like a trumpet said, "Come up here, and I will show you what must take place after this." At once I was in the Spirit, and there before me was a throne in heaven with someone sitting on it."*
– Revelation 4:1-2

When we read about John the Revelator, we see that there was a great invitation given to him by the Lord. The invitation was "come up here", and the Lord invited John through the open door! When we are spending time in the presence of the Lord, we need to become still before Him so that we can hear His invitation and RESPOND to it. (Psalm 46:10)

Remember, it is important to respond to the realm! God gives us a window of opportunity.

We don't hesitate. We don't delay. When God speaks, we respond!

### 4. Faith Activates - Don't Wait For A Sovereign Move!

- Romans 5:12

- Habakkuk 2:4

Every time I worship I find myself being able to activate my faith for heavenly encounter. Look to see what the bible says about your praise and worship in Psalm 22:3…

**APPLICATIONS FOR HOME**

**1. Spend Devotional Time "Before" The Lord.**

In Psalm 16:8, King David said "I have set the Lord continually before me; because He is at my right hand, I will not be shaken." It is possible to spend time "at his feet". We do this as we simply come before Him. As you spend time in His presence recognizing His greatness, you will begin to find yourself moving into a greater realm of boldness in the spirit. Focus on these scriptures:

- Matthew 5:35
- Psalm 132:7
- Psalm 99:5
- James 4:8

**2. Worship into the Heavens.**

Purpose to praise and worship until you find yourself in the heavens. Once you are there, begin to take notice of what God is speaking or showing. Make sure to journal your experiences – so that you can reflect upon them and watch them increase and expand!

**3. Receive "Heavenly Downloads"**

Because Heaven is the realm of creativity, begin to ask God for heavenly downloads… new ideas, inventions, creations, paintings, job skills, wisdom, etc. As you spend more time in the heavens you will be more effective here on the earth!

# RECOMMENDED RESOURCES:

## CDs

**Heavenly Things: Throne Room Encounters**
By Joshua Mills
Released by PIP Media Group
P.O. Box 4037
Palm Springs, CA 92263

All resources are available online at:
www.NewWineInternational.org

The Intensified Glory Institute
School of Signs & Wonders

## Lesson #7
# FLOWING IN UNUSUAL SIGNS & WONDERS

**Course I - Lesson 7**

**FLOWING IN UNUSUAL SIGNS & WONDERS**

**Objective:** To consider biblical signs and wonders and gain practical understanding in "how to flow" with this miraculous aspect of the glory realm.

**Overview:** Within this lesson we will search the scriptures and find out what the Word of God says about flowing in unusual signs and wonders:

- Understanding the Signs

- Understanding the Wonders

- Signs & Wonders in the Bible

- Why Does God Send Signs & Wonders?

- You Can Do It Too!

- Modern Day Signs & Wonders

- Electricity Of The Spirit

**SCRIPTURES FOR MEDITATION:**

☐ John 14:12

☐ Acts 8:6-8

☐ Acts 2:17-21

The Intensified Glory Institute ——————— NOTES

 **HIDDEN REVELATION**

## UNDERSTANDING THE SIGNS

Here is a dictionary definition of the word "Sign"
1. A token, indication
2. Any object, event or pattern that conveys a meaning
3. A conventional or arbitrary mark used as an abbreviation for the word or words it represents.
4. A notice, direction, warning that is displayed for public view.

In the bible "Signs" take place in the earth. (Acts 2:19)

Example: Road Signs or Directional Signs

**Don't stop at the sign... keep going!**

## FACTS ABOUT SIGNS

1. God's signs have a voice and carry a specific message. Exodus 4:8
2. During Jesus' ministry people expected a performance of signs as proof of supernatural authority. Matthew 16:1
3. Signs will accompany those who believe. Mark 16:17
4. Signs mark true apostles. 2 Corinthians 12:12
5. Signs will confirm the preaching of the Word of God. Mark 16:20

www.IntensifiedGloryInstitute.com

The Intensified Glory Institute ———————————— NOTES

## UNDERSTANDING THE WONDERS

Here is a dictionary definition of the word "Wonder"

1. Something strange and surprising; a cause of surprise, astonishment, or admiration.
2. Miraculous deed or event; remarkable phenomenon.

In the bible "Wonders" take place in the heavens. (Acts 2:19)

The Aurora Borealis in the Northern Canadian sky

## FACTS ABOUT WONDERS

1. Every occurrence of "wonders" in the bible is used with the word "signs".

2. The Lord allows signs and wonders to be done by, or through people's hands. Acts 14:3

*"Long time therefore abode they speaking boldly in the Lord, which gave testimony unto the word of his grace, and granted signs and wonders to be done by their hands."* – Acts 14:3

# SIGNS & WONDERS IN THE BIBLE

## *Old Testament*

- The Sun Stood Still – Joshua 10:12-14

- Water Flowed From A Rock – Exodus 17:6, Psalm 78:15-16

- The Red Sea Parted – Exodus 14:22, Hebrews 11:29

- An Iron Ax Floated On Water – 2 Kings 6:5-6

- Water Turned Into Blood – Exodus 7:17

- Resurrection Power – 1 Kings 17:17-23, 2 Kings 4:32-37, 2 Kings 13:21

- Aaron's Rod Blossomed – Numbers 17:1-9

- Protected From Burning In The Furnace – Daniel 3:23-27

- Supernaturally Replenished Supply Of Oil – 1 Kings 17:9-16, 2 Kings 4:2-7

- Talking Donkey – Numbers 22:23-30

- Rod Became A Serpent – Exodus 4:3-4

- The Jordan River Parted – 2 Kings 2:8

- The Sun Went Backwards – 2 Kings 20:9-11

- Manna From Heaven – Exodus 16:4-31

- Supernatural Dew – Judges 6:36-40

- Commanding Drought/Rain – 1 Kings 17:1-14, James 5:17-18

## *New Testament*

- Water Into Wine – John 2:1-11

- Walked On Water – Matthew 14:22-23, Mark 6:42-52, John 6:16-21

- Money In Fish's Mouth – Matthew 17:24-27

- Jesus Fed Multitudes with Fishes and Loaves – Matthew 16:8-10

- Fig Tree Shriveled Up At Command – Matthew 21:17-22

- Power Over Stormy Weather – Mark 6:45-52

- Resurrection Power – Luke 7:11-16, Mark 5:22-24, John 11

- Miraculous Catch Of Fish – John 21:5-12

- Unharmed by Poisonous Snakes – Mark 16:18, Luke 10:19, Acts 28:3-6

- Supernatural Prison Escape – Acts 5:17-25, Acts 16:25-40

- Power Shadow – Acts 5:15

*"And many other signs truly did Jesus in the presence of his disciples, which are not written in this book…"* – John 20:30

The Intensified Glory Institute —————————— NOTES

# WHY DOES GOD SEND SIGNS & WONDERS?

*A "sign" is supposed to make you "wonder!"*

**1. In the Old Testament, signs and wonders served as evidence of the one true God:**

- Exodus 7:17
- Deuteronomy 4:35
- Joshua 2:11
- Daniel 3:28-29

**2. God performs signs and wonders to meet the needs of His people.**

- Exodus 16:4-31
- Exodus 17:5-7
- 1 Kings 17:4-7
- 2 Kings 2:19-22
- Matthew 16:8-10

**3. Signs and Wonders increase our faith.**

- John 2:11
- Acts 9:42

**4. Signs and wonders carry a prophetic voice**

- Exodus 4:8

**5. Signs and Wonders serve as a confirmation of God's Word**

- Judges 6:11-21
- Matthew 11:2-5
- Mark 16:20

- John 5:36
- Acts 2:22, Acts 8:6

## 6. They testify that a minister or person is sent by God.

- 2 Corinthians 12:12

## MODERN DAY SIGNS & WONDERS

- Creative Miracles & Healings

- Raising The Dead

- Casting Out Demons

- Speaking In New Tongues

- Holy Laughter

- Shaking

- Falling Under The Power

- Singing In The Spirit

- Trances / Visions

- Gold Teeth / Dental Miracles

- Gold Dust

- Words Of Knowledge

## SUPERNATURAL OIL

*"...thou anointest my head with oil; my cup runneth over."* – Psalm 23:5

Supernatural Oil represents the following:

1.    Holy Spirit Anointing (Psalm 23:5, Psalm 92:10, Zechariah 4)

2.    Healing (James 5:14)

3.    Unity & Blessing (Psalm 133)

Many times when the Holy Spirit places this supernatural oil upon a person's head, hands or feet it will come along with a beautiful fragrance from heaven.

www.IntensifiedGloryInstitute.com

163

The Intensified Glory Institute ———————— NOTES

 **KEYS FOR ACTIVATION**

## YOU CAN DO IT TOO!

God has given each of us the power to perform the same signs and wonders that Jesus Christ did, if we have faith to believe for it.

*"Verily, verily, I say unto you, He that believeth on me, the works that I do shall he do also; and greater works than these shall he do; because I go unto my Father."* – John 14:12

- Matthew 10:1-8
- Mark 16:16-18

If you believe they will happen – they will!
If you don't believe they will happen – they won't!

*"...According to your faith be it unto you."* – Matthew 9:29

## ELECTRICITY OF THE SPIRIT

We must understand what the Word of God says about the power of the Spirit. If we understand that power, we will be able to harness that power and release it everywhere we go!

1. The Gospel Is The Power of God!

*"For I am not ashamed of the gospel of Christ: for it is the power of God unto salvation to every one that believeth; to the Jew first, and also to the Greek. For therein is the righteousness of God revealed from faith to faith: as it is written, The just shall live by faith."* – Romans 1:16-17

The Intensified Glory Institute ——————— NOTES

*"And they went forth, and preached every where, the Lord working with them, and confirming the word with signs following."* – Mark 16:20

The Word always works! If we speak the Word, we will release the power!

2. The Power Must Be Seen!

*"And my speech and my preaching was not with enticing words of man's wisdom, but in demonstration of the Spirit and of power."* – 1 Corinthians 2:4

3. The Power Will Be Displayed Through You!

*"But you will receive power when the Holy Spirit comes on you; and you will be my witnesses in Jerusalem, and in all Judea and Samaria, and to the ends of the earth."* – Acts 1:8 (NIV)

Declaring *signs* by faith brings the manifestation, because *signs will follow* those who *believe*.

## RECOMMENDED RESOURCES:

*DVDs*

**Covered In Glory**
With Joshua Mills
Distributed by New Wine International
P.O. Box 4037, Palm Springs, CA 92263

*Books*

**Like A Mighty Wind**
By Mel Tari, with Cliff Dudley
Published by New Leaf Press, Inc.
P.O. Box 726, Green Forest, AR  72638

**Golden Glory**
By Ruth Ward Heflin
Published by McDougal Publishing
P.O. Box 3595, Hagerstown, MD  21742

All resources are available online at:
www.NewWineInternational.org

The Intensified Glory Institute
School of Signs & Wonders

**Lesson #8**
# HOW TO OPERATE IN CREATIVE MIRACLES

**Course I - Lesson 8**

# HOW TO OPERATE IN CREATIVE MIRACLES

**Objective:** To understand the power of God that has been placed within each believer to work healings and creative miracles. In this lesson we will also become familiar with techniques and scriptural practices for divine healing.

**Overview:** Within this lesson we will search the scriptures and find out what the Word of God says about operating in creative miracles:

- Qualifications for Operating in Creative Miracles

- Understanding The Miracle Realm

- Various Styles & Techniques

- Healing Scriptures and Application

**SCRIPTURES FOR MEDITATION:**

☐ Acts 10:38

☐ John 14:12

☐ Proverbs 3:5-7

☐ Romans 4:17

☐ Matthew 15:29-31

The Intensified Glory Institute ———————————— NOTES

 **HIDDEN REVELATION**

## QUALIFICATIONS FOR OPERATING IN CREATIVE MIRACLES

1. **You Must _____**

   John 6:28

   Mark 16:17

   John 14:12

2. **You Must Be _____ with Power**

   Luke 4:18

   Acts 1:8

It is impossible to work miracles in our own strength. The dictionary says that a miracle is an effect or extraordinary event in the physical world that surpasses all known human or natural powers. It defies scientific logic and order.

We must believe the Word of God (because the Word of God becomes the power of God inside of us!). We must know what it says and stand on that truth! We must also believe that we have been anointed to work miracles in the name of Jesus Christ, by the power of the Holy Spirit.

God does the miracle, but He chooses to release it through us as we believe His Word by faith!

# WHAT DOES THE BIBLE SAY ABOUT HEALING?

<u>In the Old Testament:</u>

**Exodus 15:25-26**     *"I Am the Lord that healeth thee."*

**Deuteronomy 28:61;**
**Galatians 3:13**     Christ has redeemed us from the curse of every sickness

**Psalm 103:3**     *"...who healeth all thy diseases."*

**Isaiah 53:4-5**     *"...with His stripes we are healed."*

**Jeremiah 33:6**     *"...I will bring it health and cure, and I will cure them..."*

**Ezekiel 34:2-4,15-16**     *"...will bind up that which was broken, and will strengthen that which was sick..."*

**Malachi 4:2**     *"...the Sun of righteousness shall arise with healing in His wings."*

**Proverbs 4:20-23**     *"...My Words are life unto those that find them, and health to all their flesh."*

**Psalm 107:20**     *"He sent His Word, and healed them..."*

**Psalm 67:2**     *"That thy way may be known upon the earth, thy saving health among the nations."*

**Jeremiah 32:27**     *"I Am the Lord, the God of all flesh: is there any thing too hard for me?"*

# WHAT DOES THE BIBLE SAY ABOUT HEALING?

<u>In the New Testament:</u>

**Matthew 8:16-17**   *"…Himself took our infirmities, and bare our sicknesses."*

**Mark 16:15-18**   *"…Go ye…lay hands on the sick, and they shall recover."*

**1 Corinthians 6:13-20**   *"…your body is a temple of the Holy Spirit."*

**Romans 8:11**   *"…the Spirit of Him that raised up Jesus from the dead… shall also quicken your mortal bodies…"*

**1 Thessalonians 5:23**   *"…your whole spirit and soul and body be preserved blameless…"*

**Hebrews 13:8**   *"Jesus Christ is the same yesterday, and today, and forever."*

**James 5:14-16**   *"And the prayer of faith shall save the sick, and the Lord shall raise Him up…"*

**1 Peter 2:24**   *"…by whose stripes ye were healed."*

**3 John 2**   *"Beloved, I wish above all things that thou mayest prosper and be in health…"*

www.IntensifiedGloryInstitute.com

# UNDERSTANDING THE MIRACLE REALM

**Jesus Christ Saves and Heals All**

*"That if thou shalt confess with thy mouth the Lord Jesus, and shalt believe in thine heart that God hath raised him from the dead, thou shalt be saved."*
- Romans 10:9

    1. Steps to being saved:

        a.    _____ the Word of God.
        b.    _____ the Word in your heart.
        c.    _____ is made unto salvation.

    2. Steps to being healed:

        a.    _____ the Word of God
        b.    _____ the Word in your heart.
        c.    _____ (action) is done to confirm the healing.

The steps are the same and the results are the same. You believe and then you receive. Both require faith on the part of the receiver.

*"But without faith it is impossible to please him: for he that cometh to God must believe that he is, and that he is a rewarder of them that diligently seek him."*
– Hebrews 11:6

We are not asking God to ____ something, we are simply thanking Him for what He has already _____, and now we _____ the gift. Our faith moves the miracle from heaven to earth!

**Not All Healings Are Instant – but <u>Miracles</u> Are!**

- Luke 17:12 – the ten lepers were cleansed ___ _____ _____.

- John 9:6 – the blind man _____ _____ seeing.

- Mark 11:20 – the fig tree withered away ____ _____ _____.

## YOU MUST HAVE CONFIDENCE IN GOD

*If you lack confidence, you will lack evidence!*

We must be confident in the Word of God, and the power of His glory to bring forth the miracles. Whatever you speak to in faith, _____ obey you!

*"For verily I say unto you, That whosoever shall say unto this mountain, Be thou removed, and be thou cast into the sea; and shall not doubt in his heart, but shall believe that those things which he saith shall come to pass; he shall have whatsoever he saith."* – Mark 11:23

Jesus Christ had confidence over:

a. _____ & _____

b. _____ & _____

c. The _____ or _____

d. The _____ _____

The Intensified Glory Institute ——————————— NOTES

## TIPS FOR SUCCESS

**1. Remember, God always does the miracle – NOT YOU!**
This takes away any "pressure to perform". (Philippians 2:13)

**2. Be Natural in Being Supernatural!**
This almost seems like an oxymoron, but God wants this flow of miraculous power to be a natural occurrence in our life. Being pious won't heal the sick. Being religious won't heal the sick. Squeezing your eyes shut or making funny facial expressions will not heal the sick! Let the power of God flow "naturally" through you – He created you to operate in this way!

**3. Magnify the Works of the Lord!**
Be thankful in everything that you see the Lord do! When you witness a miracle (no matter how small it may look), be sure to give God all the glory, and magnify the works of His hand. As you magnify Him you will see the miracles continue to flow with ease. Document and record these testimonies to build faith in other believers as well.

**4. Where there is Great Love, there are always Great Miracles!**
Frances Hunter says *"Looking for feelings instead of healings can rob you of what God wants to do through you."* Remember that God's love is the greatest power available to us. It is available at all times, whether we feel it or not. If we will develop compassion for those who are sick and hurting, we will see God's love flow through us with many miracles following.

The Intensified Glory Institute ———————— NOTES

# VARIOUS STYLES & TECHNIQUES

### 1. Laying On Of Hands

- Mark 16:17-18 – Lay hands on the sick, and they shall recover.

- Mark 1:40-42 – Jesus touched the leper and he was healed!

- Mark 5:35-40 – Jesus touched the lady's hand and she was healed!

- Mark 7:32-35 – Jesus touched the deaf ears and they opened!

- Matthew 18:19 – Touch and agree for miracle healing.

There are many different techniques for laying on of hands. Some of these include praying with your hands on the person's head, on their neck, on the affected area (sometimes with your hand on top of theirs) or *"Growing Out Arms & Legs"*.

### 2. Let The Sick Lay Hands On You

- Luke 6:19 – Everyone was touching Jesus to be cured of sickness

- Mark 6:56 – As many as touched Him were made whole.

- Mark 5:25-34 – The woman with the issue of blood.

### 3. Word Of Knowledge
(this is discussed further in Course II)

- 1 Corinthians 2:12-13

### 4. Anointing With Oil

- Oil is symbolic of the Holy Spirit's anointing. (Point of contact)

- James 5:14-15 – *"Is any sick... anoint him with oil..."*

- Mark 6:12-13 – *"...anointed with oil many that were sick..."*

### 5. Healing Through Intercessory Prayer

- Matthew 8:5-13 – Healed at a distance.

### 6. Healing Through Use Of Prayer Cloths

- Acts 19:11-12 – Extraordinary miracles through Paul.

### 7. Faith In Action

- Luke 6:6-10 – Stretched forth hand in obedience.

- John 9:1-7 – Blind man put faith into action by washing in the pool.

    a. Responding to the Realm (30-40 seconds)

    b. Running Into the Miracle Realm
       (from natural → supernatural)

    c. Supernatural Weight-loss – Check 7 Times!
       (The leper dipped 7 times – 2 Kings 5:1-14)

    d. Doing Something You Could Not Do
       (Mark 2:10-12, Mark 3:5, Mark 8:23-25)

## 8. Falling Down

The scriptures teach three kinds of *"falling down"* before the Lord:

a. **Voluntary**
(Example: fall on our knees in worship, Luke 17:16 or "soaking" before the Lord in prayer)

b. **Under A Heavy Burden Of Prayer**
(Example: Jesus in Gethsemane, Matthew 26:36-39)

c. **Under The Power**
(Example:  The scriptures below)

• John 18:1-6 – The power made a group of men fall to the ground!

• Matthew 28:1-4 – Soldiers became as "dead men" and fell down.

• Matthew 17:1-6 – The disciples fell on their face.

• Acts 9:4 – Saul had an encounter with the Lord and fell down.

• Ezekiel 1:28 – Ezekiel had a heavenly encounter.

• 2 Chronicles 5:13-14 – The priests could not stand to minister.

Miracles that have manifested by falling "Under The Power":

• Healing from Bareness *(recommended resource: "Childbirth In The Glory" CD & Book by Janet Angela Mills)*

• Brand New Heart, Lower Discs Recreated in Back, Restored Sight, Dental Miracles, Supernatural Weight-loss, etc.

• Healings In Marriages

## 9. Holy Laughter

- Ecclesiastes 3:4 – A time to weep and a time to laugh

- Proverbs 15:13 – A glad heart will change your countenance!

- Proverbs 17:22 – Laughter does good just like a medicine!

- Proverbs 18:14 – What's on the inside will manifest on the outside.

## 10. Miracles In The Glory

- 2 Chronicles 5:13-14 – The cloud of glory covered them all.

- The Children of Israel found miracles within the glory cloud.

- Acts 4:29-31 – The hand of God wrought many miracles.

## MINISTERING MIRACLES ONE-ON-ONE

Remember that sickness is a spirit, and you must command that spirit to leave the physical body of the person you are ministering to. You can also command the person's body to come into alignment with the healing Word of God.

Here is a sample prayer for when I minister personally with someone in the miraculous:

*"Father, in the name of Jesus, I thank You for releasing Your healing virtue upon my (brother/sister). I command every spirit of (name the sickness) to go in the name of Jesus Christ, by the power of the Holy Spirit. I command this body to be made whole in the name of Jesus, by the power of Your glory."*

We should always pray in this way:

- ➢ To the Father

- ➢ In the name of Jesus Christ

- ➢ By the power of the Holy Spirit

## MAKING ROOM FOR THE TESTIMONY

*"And they overcame him by the blood of the Lamb, and by the word of their testimony; and they loved not their lives unto the death."* – Revelation 12:11

When ministering in miracles within a corporate setting, we must always make room for the testimony. We must give people an opportunity to stand in front of others and profess the goodness of God. Jesus Christ set this example for us in Luke 6:8. Jesus asked the man with the withered hand to stand up in front of others so that they could all see the miracle.

| THE TESTIMONY BUILDS FOUR REALMS | |
|---|---|
| #1 | |
| #2 | |
| #3 | |
| #4 | |

*The testimony builds faith, plants seeds and produces more miracles!*

This is the nature of the testimony. We have seen this time and time again. When operating in creative miracles in a corporate setting it is very important to allow time for the testimony to be shared. It is like fuel for the Holy Spirit fire… the testimonies will cause the miracles to be set *ABLAZE!*

An entire CD teaching about the *"Power Of Your Testimony"* is available by visiting our online bookstore at: www.newwineinternational.org

## GOD HEALS BACK PAIN!

Statistics show that over 80% of the world is suffering with back problems!

This might seem like a big problem, but we serve a BIG God, and He lives inside of you!  God wants to use you as a modern day wonderworker for His glory!

Here are a few keys on how to minister to those with back pains:

## BACK PAIN

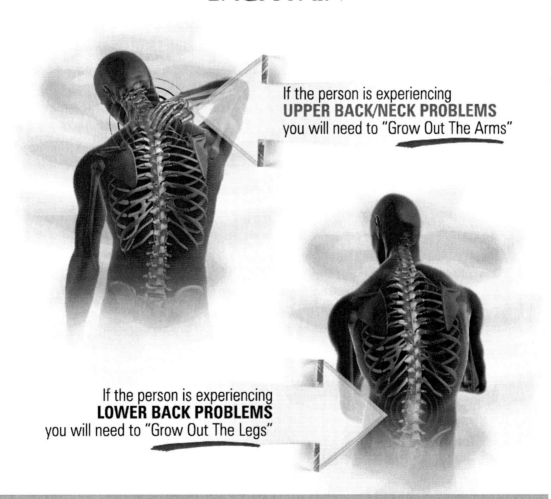

If the person is experiencing **UPPER BACK/NECK PROBLEMS** you will need to "Grow Out The Arms"

If the person is experiencing **LOWER BACK PROBLEMS** you will need to "Grow Out The Legs"

Statistics show that over **80% of the world** is suffering with back problems!

www.IntensifiedGloryInstitute.com

# GROWING OUT ARMS

*Give these 7-step instructions to the person you're ministering to as they are facing you:*

**STEP 1:**

STEP 1:
Stand up straight, with your toes even and feet together

**STEP 2:**
Extend your arms in front of you with the palms facing each other, about a half-inch apart.

**STEP 3:**
Stretch your arms straight out as far as you can

**STEP 4:**
Bring your hands tightly together and hold them in this way until you bend your elbows so that you can see the ends of your fingers. If the arms are uneven, the fingers of the long arm will extend beyond the fingers of the shorter arm.

**STEP 5:**
Stretch your arms out again with your hands lighting touching each other.

**STEP 6:**
Command the short arm to grow. Speak to the other parts as well: "Spine, muscles, nerves, ligaments and tendons, be adjusted in the name of Jesus."

**STEP 7:**
Thank God for it - and watch the miracle happen before your eyes!

**STEP 4:**

**STEP 5:**

**STEP 7:**

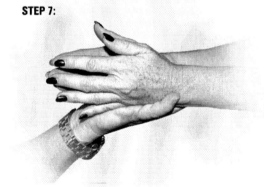

The Intensified Glory Institute ———————————— NOTES

# GROWING OUT LEGS

*Give these 4-step instructions to the person you're ministering to as they sit with their back straight up in a chair facing you:*

**STEP 1:**
Have them lift up their legs straight out in front of them. They may need your help to do this. Always be very careful when lifting their legs as sometimes this can be painful. DO NOT force legs!

**STEP 2:**
You will be able to look and see if there is a difference in length by viewing the bottoms of the shoes or by putting your thumbs on the ankle bone (as pictured in the photo →).

**STEP 3:**
Hold the feet lightly in your hands and command the back to align itself. Command the short leg to grow out in the name of Jesus, and by the power of the Holy Spirit!

**STEP 4:**
Thank God for it and watch the miracle happen before your eyes! Many times in the glory you will see the miracle happen just as you simply begin to pray - even before you finish your prayer!

**STEP 1:**

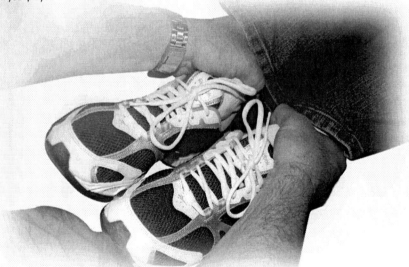

# HINDRANCES TO RECEIVING MIRACLES FROM GOD

Sometimes when healing does not occur instantly, there are hindrances that can be discovered and dealt with so that healing miracles can be received.

You will usually be able to determine the hindrance that is present by asking the person a few brief questions.

Some examples:

> *Did someone cause this condition?  Have you forgiven them?*

> *Did you experience a traumatic event prior to when this condition started?*
(Feelings of guilt, shame or grief may cause illness)

> *Did you know about this condition before the doctor told you?*
(Sometimes illness is caused by word curses being spoken into existence)

Sometimes a parent, sibling or friend accompanying the sick person may speak of it.  Always keep your eyes and ears open to see and hear what the Spirit of God is revealing:

1. **Unforgiveness**

   *"For if ye forgive men their trespasses, your heavenly Father will also forgive you: But if ye forgive not men their trespasses, neither will your Father forgive your trespasses."* – Matthew 6:14-15

2. **Resentment, Anger, Bitterness**

### 3. Natural Mind

*"And my speech and my preaching was not with enticing words of man's wisdom, but in demonstration of the Spirit and of power… But the natural man receiveth not the things of the Spirit of God: for they are foolishness unto him: neither can he know them, because they are spiritually discerned."* – 1 Corinthians 2:4, 14

- Your natural mind cannot figure out how washing your eyes in the pool or spitting on the ground and putting mud on blind eyes causes them to see. Dipping in the Jordan river 7 times to get rid of leprosy, even being told to "pick up your bed and walk" when you are paralyzed.

### 4. Hardness Of Heart

*"Afterward he appeared unto the eleven as they sat at meat, and upbraided them with their unbelief and hardness of heart, because they believed not them which had seen him after he was risen."* – Mark 16:14

### 5. A Curse

*"Christ hath redeemed us from the curse of the law, being made a curse for us: for it is written, Cursed is every one that hangeth on a tree."* – Galatians 3:13

*"For the law of the Spirit of life in Christ Jesus hath made me free from the law of sin and death."* – Romans 8:2

- Must be taught that the <u>curse</u> has been broken. No more lies.

### 6. Past or Current Involvement In The Occult

- Freemasonry Within Family

7. **Lack of Desire For Healing**

*"Be sober, be vigilant; because your adversary the devil, as a roaring lion, walketh about, seeking whom he may devour." – 1 Peter 5:8*

8. **Religious Spirits**

*"For the kingdom of God is not in word, but in power."*
- 1 Corinthians 4:20

*"Having a form of godliness, but denying the power thereof: from such turn away." – 2 Timothy 3:5*

- Unbelief That God Heals Today (Matthew 17:19, Mark 6:5)

9. **Fear**

*"Fear not, daughter of Sion: behold, thy King cometh…" - John 12:15*

*"But even the very hairs of your head are all numbered. Fear not therefore: ye are of more value than many sparrows." - Luke 12:7,*

*"Fear them not therefore: for there is nothing covered, that shall not be revealed; and hid, that shall not be known." - Matthew 10:26*

10. **Unresolved Guilt**

*"In whom we have redemption through his blood, the forgiveness of sins, according to the riches of his grace." - Ephesians 1:7*

11. **Disobedience / Sin**

*"If my people, which are called by my name, shall humble themselves, and pray, and seek my face, and turn from their wicked ways; then will I hear from heaven, and will forgive their sin, and will heal their land."*
- 2 Chronicles 7:14

12. **Ungodly Soul Ties**

13. **Belief That God Brought The Sickness**

*"But if the Spirit of him that raised up Jesus from the dead dwell in you, he that raised up Christ from the dead shall also quicken your mortal bodies by his Spirit that dwelleth in you."* - Romans 8:11

*"He sent his word, and healed them, and delivered them from their destructions."* - Psalm 107:20

14. **Demonic Spirit of Illness or Affliction**

*"And these signs shall follow them that believe; In my name shall they cast out devils…"* – Mark 16:17

The Intensified Glory Institute ———————————— NOTES

 **KEYS FOR ACTIVATION**

## SIMPLE KEYS FOR MINISTERING TO THE SICK

1. **Find out the problem/condition**
   *(Sometimes the Lord will reveal this to you by a word of knowledge, at other times you may ask someone if they are in need of healing)*

2. **TEACH → PREACH → HEAL**

3. **Decide which healing method to use and do it!**
   Command the sickness to go and the body to be made whole. *(Always praying in the name of Jesus, by the power of the Holy Spirit).*

4. **Ask the recipient to "do something they couldn't do before" and look for the miracle!**

www.IntensifiedGloryInstitute.com

## PHYSICAL BODY
# HEALING SCRIPTURES

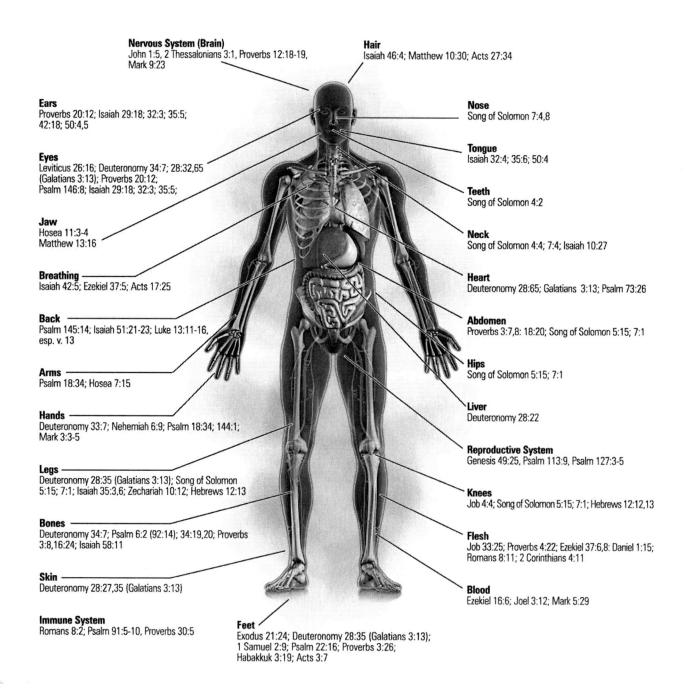

**Nervous System (Brain)**
John 1:5, 2 Thessalonians 3:1, Proverbs 12:18-19, Mark 9:23

**Hair**
Isaiah 46:4; Matthew 10:30; Acts 27:34

**Ears**
Proverbs 20:12; Isaiah 29:18; 32:3; 35:5; 42:18; 50:4,5

**Eyes**
Leviticus 26:16; Deuteronomy 34:7; 28:32,65 (Galatians 3:13); Proverbs 20:12; Psalm 146:8; Isaiah 29:18; 32:3; 35:5;

**Jaw**
Hosea 11:3-4
Matthew 13:16

**Breathing**
Isaiah 42:5; Ezekiel 37:5; Acts 17:25

**Back**
Psalm 145:14; Isaiah 51:21-23; Luke 13:11-16, esp. v. 13

**Arms**
Psalm 18:34; Hosea 7:15

**Hands**
Deuteronomy 33:7; Nehemiah 6:9; Psalm 18:34; 144:1; Mark 3:3-5

**Legs**
Deuteronomy 28:35 (Galatians 3:13); Song of Solomon 5:15; 7:1; Isaiah 35:3,6; Zechariah 10:12; Hebrews 12:13

**Bones**
Deuteronomy 34:7; Psalm 6:2 (92:14); 34:19,20; Proverbs 3:8,16:24; Isaiah 58:11

**Skin**
Deuteronomy 28:27,35 (Galatians 3:13)

**Immune System**
Romans 8:2; Psalm 91:5-10, Proverbs 30:5

**Nose**
Song of Solomon 7:4,8

**Tongue**
Isaiah 32:4; 35:6; 50:4

**Teeth**
Song of Solomon 4:2

**Neck**
Song of Solomon 4:4; 7:4; Isaiah 10:27

**Heart**
Deuteronomy 28:65; Galatians 3:13; Psalm 73:26

**Abdomen**
Proverbs 3:7,8: 18:20; Song of Solomon 5:15; 7:1

**Hips**
Song of Solomon 5:15; 7:1

**Liver**
Deuteronomy 28:22

**Reproductive System**
Genesis 49:25, Psalm 113:9, Psalm 127:3-5

**Knees**
Job 4:4; Song of Solomon 5:15; 7:1; Hebrews 12:12,13

**Flesh**
Job 33:25; Proverbs 4:22; Ezekiel 37:6,8; Daniel 1:15; Romans 8:11; 2 Corinthians 4:11

**Blood**
Ezekiel 16:6; Joel 3:12; Mark 5:29

**Feet**
Exodus 21:24; Deuteronomy 28:35 (Galatians 3:13); 1 Samuel 2:9; Psalm 22:16; Proverbs 3:26; Habakkuk 3:19; Acts 3:7

198

Course I – Lesson 8

# HOW TO OPERATE IN CREATIVE MIRACLES

| **SCRIPTURE REFERENCES I** | |
|---|---|
| **Scriptures Pertaining To Specific Parts Of The Body** | |
| **Abdomen** *(Belly/Intestines/Stomach)* | Proverbs 3:8<br>Proverbs 18:20<br>Deuteronomy 28:27[4] (Galatians 3:13)<br>Acts 28:8,9 |
| **Ankles** | 1 Samuel 2:9<br>Psalm 121:3 |
| **Back** | Psalm 145:14<br>Leviticus 21:18-23<br>Luke 13:11-16 |
| **Blood** | Joel 3:21<br>Ezekiel 16:6<br>Mark 5:29 |
| **Bones** | Proverbs 3:8<br>Isaiah 58:11<br>Psalm 34:19-20<br>Acts 3:6-7 |
| **Brain** | John 14:26<br>Psalm 119:16<br>Isaiah 11:2-3 |
| **Breathing** | Genesis 2:7 |
| **Digestion** | Psalm 22:26<br>Matthew 15:17<br>Ecclesiastes 3:13 |

---

[4] All scriptures within Deuteronomy, Chapter 28 must be understood along with Galatians 3:13 which states that *"Christ redeemed us from the curse of the law by becoming a curse for us…".* Jesus Christ endured sickness and death on the cross of Calvary so that we can freely receive health and healing.

# SCRIPTURE REFERENCES II

| Scriptures Pertaining To Specific Parts Of The Body | |
| --- | --- |
| **Ears** | Proverbs 20:12<br>Isaiah 35:5<br>Isaiah 29:18<br>Isaiah 32:3 |
| **Eyes** | Proverbs 20:12<br>Psalm 146:8<br>Isaiah 29:18<br>Isaiah 35:4-5<br>Isaiah 32:3<br>Deuteronomy 34:7<br>Matthew 13:16 |
| **Feet** | 1 Samuel 2:9<br>Psalm 91:11-12<br>Psalm 121:3<br>Proverbs 3:23,26<br>Acts 3:7<br>Acts 14:8,10<br>Habakkuk 3:19 |
| **Flesh** | Proverbs 4:22<br>Job 33:24-25<br>Ezekiel 37:6<br>2 Corinthians 4:11<br>Daniel 1:15<br>Jeremiah 32:27 |
| **Groin** | Deuteronomy 28:27 (Galatians 3:13)<br>Proverbs 31:17<br>Ephesians 6:14 |

## SCRIPTURE REFERENCES III

| Scriptures Pertaining To Specific Parts Of The Body | |
|---|---|
| **Hair** | Luke 21:18 |
| | Luke 12:7 |
| | 2 Samuel 14:11 |
| | 2 Samuel 25 |
| **Hands** | Deuteronomy 33:7 |
| | Job 4:3 |
| | Nehemiah 6:9 |
| | Psalm 144:1 |
| | Isaiah 41:13 |
| | Isaiah 35:3 |
| | Mark 3:3,5 |
| **Heart** | Psalm 73:26 |
| | Deuteronomy 28:61,65 (Galatians 3:13) |
| | Psalm 147:3 |
| | Psalm 22:26 |
| | Psalm 27:14 |
| **Immune System** | Romans 8:2 |
| | Psalm 91:5-10 |
| | Exodus 11:7 |
| | Psalm 3:3 |
| | Isaiah 4:4,5 |
| | Proverbs 30:5 |
| | Deuteronomy 28:21 (Galatians 3:13) |
| **Jaw** | Hosea 11:3,4 |
| **Kidneys** | Deuteronomy 28:61 (Galatians 3:13) |
| **Knees** | Job 4:4 |
| | Isaiah 35:3 |
| | Hebrews 12:12 |

# SCRIPTURE REFERENCES IV

| Scriptures Pertaining To Specific Parts Of The Body ||
|---|---|
| **Legs** | Isaiah 35:6<br>1 Samuel 2:4<br>Zechariah 10:12<br>Hebrews 12:13<br>Deuteronomy 28:35 (Galatians 3:13) |
| **Liver** | Deuteronomy 28:22 (Galatians 3:13) |
| **Mouth**<br>*(Gums/Lips/Taste Buds/Tongue)* | Psalm 103:5<br>Proverbs 12:18-19<br>Proverbs 8:6-8<br>Psalm 51:15<br>Job 6:6,30 |
| **Neck** | Isaiah 10:27 |
| **Nervous System** *(Brain)* | John 1:5<br>2 Thessalonians 3:1<br>Proverbs 12:28<br>Isaiah 58:8,12<br>Luke 1:37<br>Luke 18:27<br>Mark 9:23<br>Jeremiah 32:27<br>Deuteronomy 28:61 (Galatians 3:13)<br>Galatians 3:13 |
| **Nose** | Genesis 2:7<br>Song of Songs 7:4,8 |
| **Reproductive System** | Genesis 49:25<br>Exodus 23:26<br>Psalm 113:9<br>Psalm 127:3-5<br>Deuteronomy 7:9,12-15 |

## SCRIPTURE REFERENCES V

| Scriptures Pertaining To Specific Parts Of The Body | |
| --- | --- |
| **Respiratory System** | Genesis 2:7<br>Acts 17:25<br>Isaiah 42:5<br>Ezekiel 37:5<br>Lamentations 3:56<br>Deuteronomy 28:22, 61 (Galatians 3:13) |
| **Shoulder** | Isaiah 10:27<br>Isaiah 9:4 |
| **Sinews**<br>*(Muscles, Tendons, Ligaments, Connective Tissue)* | Job 10:11-12<br>Deuteronomy 28:27,35 (Galatians 3:13) |
| **Teeth** | Deuteronomy 34:7<br>Song of Songs 4:2-3 |
| **Tongue** | Proverbs 12:18<br>Song of Songs 4:11 |
| **Veins** | Deuteronomy 28:61 (Galatians 3:13) |

203

## RECOMMENDED RESOURCES:

**How To Heal The Sick**
By Charles & Frances Hunter
Published by Whitaker House
1030 Hunt Valley Circle, New Kensington, PA 15068

**Handbook For Healing**
By Charles & Frances Hunter
Published by Whitaker House
1030 Hunt Valley Circle, New Kensington, PA 15068

**Personal Ministry Prayer Manual**
By Joshua & Janet Angela Mills
Published by New Wine International, Inc.
P.O. Box 4037, Palm Springs, CA 92263

**Childbirth In The Glory: Declarations & Prayers**
By Janet Angela Mills
Published by New Wine International, Inc.
P.O. Box 4037, Palm Springs, CA 92263

**Power To Heal**
By Joan Hunter
Published by Whitaker House
1030 Hunt Valley Circle, New Kensington, PA 15068

All resources are available online at:
www.NewWineInternational.org

The Intensified Glory Institute
School of Signs & Wonders

## Lesson #9
# TRANSPORT IN THE SPIRIT

## Course I - Lesson 9

## TRANSPORT IN THE SPIRIT

**Objective:**  To explore scriptural accounts of supernatural transport and begin to position ourselves for this same dimension of glory.

**Overview:**  Within this lesson we will search the scriptures and find out what the Word of God says about transport in the Spirit:

- The Difference Between Truth and Fact.

- Facts About Flying

- What Is Translation In The Spirit?

- Biblical Accounts Of Translation

- What Is Transport In The Spirit?

- Biblical Examples Of Spirit Transport

- Other Supernatural Transportation

**SCRIPTURES FOR MEDITATION:**

☐ Psalm 3:3

☐ Isaiah 40:31

☐ Revelation 4:1-4

The Intensified Glory Institute ——————————— NOTES

## HIDDEN REVELATION

## THE DIFFERENCE BETWEEN TRUTH AND FACTS

- Facts are always subject to truth (Facts are fleeting)

- Truth does not change (Truth is eternal) – Malachi 3:6

- Facts can withhold information

- Truth will set you free! – John 8:32

Example:  Business Meeting at 9am

We need to move from the "natural" zone into the "supernatural" zone.

- In the world, but not confined to its realm – John 17:13-16

## WHAT IS THE TRUTH?

- God's Word is truth – John 17:17-18

- Jesus Christ is truth – John 14:6

*Revelation moves you into a higher dimension.*

- Walk and live in the truth – Psalm 86:11

- Desire truth in your inner being – Psalm 51:6

- Ask the Spirit of Truth to lead you into all truth – John 16:13

www.IntensifiedGloryInstitute.com

The Intensified Glory Institute ———————— NOTES

## WHAT DOES GOD'S WORD SAY?

In the presence of God we step into another zone – out of the natural and into the realm of revelation and truth.

- You can FLY! – Isaiah 40:31

- Ezekiel flew! – Ezekiel 1, 3:12-14

- We can live in the glory – Psalm 15:1-2

## FACTS ABOUT FLYING

You say you can't fly?  Don't be a chicken!

- The longest recorded flight of a chicken is 13 seconds

- Longest chicken flight distance: 301 ½ feet

- Eagle's have wide long wings that help them stay in the air.

- A Bald Eagle's wing span is normally 8 feet

## FEAR NOT

**Do Not Be _____-full – Be _____ Filled!**

When God desires to bring us into supernatural experience, mankind has a tendency towards being fearful of anything "unknown".  Instead of being full of fear, we need to "believe only" and become full of faith!

- Genesis 15:1 – I am thy shield

- Luke 2:10 – Angel appeared and said "Fear Not"

- Luke 8:50 – Jesus said "fear not" and "believe only"

- Revelation 1:10 – John was in the Spirit

- 2 Timothy 1:7 – *"For God hath not given us a spirit of fear, but of power, and of love, and of a sound mind."*

## WHAT IS TRANSLATION IN THE SPIRIT?

Translation is when your spirit man is being carried away into a supernatural experience (your spirit visits the third heaven or physical places on earth). Your body remains in the earth, as your spirit travels. When traveling in this way, oftentimes the body is unseen as you achieve a viewpoint from the spiritual dimension. This is not a self initiated event, but rather an experience given by the Holy Spirit and covered by the blood of Jesus Christ. Your spirit man is very active and can be trained to be alert during this supernatural experience.

- Ezekiel 3:12-14, 8:1-6, 11:1-2, 37:1-4, 43:5-6

- 2 Corinthians 12:2-4

In a translation experience, God is able to move your spirit into past, present or future locations.

## THE SILVER CORD

Sometimes during a translation experience, the person will see a silver cord which connects their spirit man with their physical body.

*"Remember your creator before the silver cord is loosed, or the golden bowl is broken, or the pitcher shattered at the fountain, or the wheel broken at the well."*
– Ecclesiastes 12:6 (NKJV)

212

This verse of scripture accurately translates the Hebrew meaning by giving us a picture of the various ways a man can die. Some people believe the golden bowl is the head (head injury); the pitcher is the lungs (lung disease) and the wheel is the heart and circulatory system (heart failure). But the most interesting one is the "silver cord." This is the only place in scripture where this term is used.

The Hebrew word for "loosed" has the idea of being removed far away. This is not the spinal cord. It appears to be describing the departure of the spirit of a man. When a man dies, his spirit also departs.

Again, the Lord speaks about drawing us closer to Him by these "cords of a man":

*"I drew them with cords of a man, with bands of love, and I was to them as one who lifts up and eases the yoke..."* – Hosea 11:4 (AMP)

Many people have these experiences of being carried out of their physical bodies, but many people don't want to talk about it – for fear!

## SLEEP WALKING & TALKING

Often times when you hear somebody talking in their sleep it sounds like a foreign language or it is difficult to understand. At times the body will begin reacting to the experience that the spirit man is encountering. This is the same with "sleep walking." The bible says that we *"walk by faith!"*

Many of these translation experiences will occur during the night hours as our bodies are in a rested position which allows our spirits to be more sensitive to the leading of the Holy Spirit. Our spirit simply follows as we're being led by faith.

This is why God desires that we would enter into the "rest" of the Glory – that we may be used at all times in all locations. We must become more sensitive to the guidance and direction of the Holy Spirit.

The Intensified Glory Institute ——————————— NOTES

## REMEMBERING LOCATIONS

Sometimes you will remember locations, people, atmospheres – days, months or even years after the initial experience happened.

What the world calls *"Déjà vu"* is what John the Revelator was speaking about in Revelation 4, when the Spirit of God called him up to *"show him things to come."*

## GOD WANTS TO SHOW YOU THINGS TO COME!

- Revelation 21:10 – John translated to see the heavenly city

Many times people will experience a sudden jolt, and wake up from these experiences when fear begins to set in. Do not be afraid!

## ACCOUNTS OF TRANSLATION IN THE SPIRIT

- Ezekiel 37 – Prophetic Experience (To show God's intent)

- Ezekiel 40:2 – Translated to "see"

- 2 Corinthians 12:2 – Paul said *"in the body or out of the body, I don't know"*

## WHAT IS TRANSPORT IN THE SPIRIT?

This is different than "translation" in the Spirit, as the physical body is lifted into a supernatural experience where the person travels without the confinements of time or distance. When traveling in this way the person's physical body will be noticeable to those around it. Often times, others will not even realize that this person is being supernaturally transported – as they will appear fully in their human form. God's purposes are accomplished in this way by supernatural means.

The Intensified Glory Institute ———————————— NOTES

# EXAMPLES OF TRANSPORT IN THE SPIRIT

- Ezekiel 8:3 – God stretched out His hand and lifted Ezekiel by his hair between earth and heaven!

- 1 Kings 18:11 – Elijah was translated and transported so frequently, it was common knowledge.

- Acts 8:39 – Philip was "caught up" while baptizing the Ethiopian.

In this passage of scripture we read about the Spirit of God transporting Philip supernaturally about 25 miles away to Azotus! The Greek word for "caught away" is harpadzo[5], which means: to seize; catch away; pluck; pull or take away by force.

- John 6:21 – Jesus, His disciples and the entire ship were transported!

This testimony documents an amazing miracle as Jesus and his twelve disciples were instantly transported IN THEIR SHIP approximately two miles across the sea to the shore!

- Luke 24:31 – Jesus vanished from sight as He was transported.

- John 20:19 – Jesus walked through the walls

- Hebrews 11:5-6 – by faith Enoch was taken from this life.

We use our faith to believe for God's perfect will to be done in our lives. It is this faith walk that will catapult us into divine supernatural experiences. Every day we believe for Him to order our footsteps and guide us along His path of righteousness.

---

[5] Reference information from Dake's Annotated Reference Bible.

# OTHER SUPERNATURAL TRANSPORTATION

- Matthew 14:26 – Jesus walks on the water

- Revelation 1:7 – Coming in a cloud

- Psalm 68:17 – Thousands of Chariots

*"The chariots of God are twenty thousand,*
*even thousands of angels:*
*the Lord is among them, as in Sinai,*
*in the holy place."*
– Psalm 68:17

# KEYS FOR ACTIVATION

Here are some scriptural keys for positioning yourself to experience transport and translation in the Spirit.

### 1. Yield Yourself To Be Used Of God

If we make room for God we will always find ourselves being used in great and mighty ways!

### 2. See It By Faith

See it in the Word and see it in the Spirit.

### 3. Believe It By Faith

As Christians we must realize that we have <u>ALL</u> experienced a supernatural translation in the Spirit by faith.

- Colossians 1:12-15

The bible says that we were translated from _____ into _____.

Our spirit translated into a glorious dimension of God's Spirit! Our soul (mind, will, conscious and emotions) and physical body caught up later!

How did this happen? We heard the Word and we believed the Word.

- James 1:22-25

We must not just hear the Word, but ACTIVELY CHOOSE to do it also!

"The just shall live by faith." (Habakkuk 2:4, Romans 1:17, Galatians 3:11)

www.IntensifiedGloryInstitute.com

## RECOMMENDED RESOURCES:

*CDs*

**Translation & Heaven's Transportation**
By Joshua Mills
Distributed by PIP Media Group
P.O. Box 4037
Palm Springs, CA 92263

All resources are available online at:
www.NewWineInternational.org

The Intensified Glory Institute
School of Signs & Wonders

## Lesson #10
# HOW TO RECEIVE
# BLESSING, FAVOR & INCREASE

## Course I - Lesson 10

## HOW TO RECEIVE BLESSING, FAVOR & INCREASE

**Objective:** To better understand the dimensions of supernatural blessing, favor and increase that God desires to place on the life of every wonder worker.

**Overview:** Within this lesson we will search the scriptures and find out what the Word of God says about miraculous blessing, favor and increase:

- The Three Realms of Giving

- The Tithe

- The Offering

- The Seed

- Keys To Supernatural Blessing

- Financial Miracles In The Glory!

**SCRIPTURES FOR MEDITATION:**

☐ Malachi 3:6-12

☐ Luke 6:38

☐ 2 Corinthians 9:6-15

223

The Intensified Glory Institute ——————————— NOTES

# HIDDEN REVELATION

*"Then said Jesus to those Jews which believed on him, If ye continue in my word, then are ye my disciples indeed; And ye shall know the truth, and the truth shall make you free."* – John 8:31-32

Your heavenly account is important and the kingdom of God must take first place in your life. As you live to minister unto the Lord, He desires that you would prosper and be blessed to be a blessing!

One of the greatest revelations I have ever received in ministry is the revelation of supernatural blessing, favor and increase.

When you are **blessed** of the Lord, it doesn't matter what it looks like in the natural, because *YOU ARE _____*!

When you have **favor** on your life, it doesn't matter what others say about you, because *YOU HAVE _____*!

When you live in the **increase**, it doesn't matter when people try to rip you off and steal from you, because *YOU HAVE _____*! It's spilling out and overflowing in your life because you are walking in divine revelation from heaven, and God's revelation never fails!

The terms "Give, giving, and gave" are mentioned _____ times in the King James Bible! God has something important to tell you about your finances.

*"Though one may be overpowered, two can defend themselves. A cord of three strands is not quickly broken."* – Ecclesiastes 4:12

Let's ask the Lord for His revelation as we begin to explore these three realms of miraculous blessing, favor and increase.

The Intensified Glory Institute ———————————— NOTES

# THE TITHE – THE REALM OF BLESSING

*"For I am the LORD, I change not; therefore ye sons of Jacob are not consumed. Even from the days of your fathers ye are gone away from mine ordinances, and have not kept them. Return unto me, and I will return unto you, saith the LORD of hosts. But ye said, Wherein shall we return? Will a man rob God? Yet ye have robbed me. But ye say, Wherein have we robbed thee? In tithes and offerings. Ye are cursed with a curse: for ye have robbed me, even this whole nation. Bring ye all the tithes into the storehouse, that there may be meat in mine house, and prove me now herewith, saith the LORD of hosts, if I will not open you the windows of heaven, and pour you out a blessing, that there shall not be room enough to receive it. And I will rebuke the devourer for your sakes, and he shall not destroy the fruits of your ground; neither shall your vine cast her fruit before the time in the field, saith the LORD of hosts. And all nations shall call you blessed: for ye shall be a delightsome land, saith the LORD of hosts."* – Malachi 3:6-12

*What is it?*

The tithe has been established by God and it is set at _____ _____ of what we receive.

Some people ask the question about whether this is before or after taxes. It always amazes me how many Christians would like to get away with as much blessing as than can, for the littlest effort. Isn't this the fleshly nature? If you're already asking this question, then you're probably looking for some loop hole in God's system of tithing.

God says bring the WHOLE tithe into the storehouse. That means ten percent of everything that you have. All that you earn, all that you're gifted with, everything that comes into your hands!

Just because the government has decided to take their share before it comes into your hands, doesn't mean that ten percent of that doesn't belong to God!

Remember, we are supposed to pay our tithe first, before we pay for anything else

The Intensified Glory Institute ——————— NOTES

## WE ROB GOD FOR TEN CENTS!

- Esau sold Jacob his inheritance for a bowl of soup
- Many Christians sell the blessing of God on their lives for ten cents!

## PEOPLE OF A NEW COVENANT

*"Christ hath redeemed us from the curse of the law, being made a curse for us: for it is written, Cursed is every one that hangeth on a tree."* – Galatians 3:13

Tithing is not under the law, but it is a spiritual pattern.

*Tithing is a pattern of faith.*

Abraham understood this spiritual principle and he put it into practice by tithing to King Melchizedeck four hundred years before Moses and the law! We must understand that tithing wasn't a practice that came with the law, but it was a spiritual pattern that God had put into order from the days of Abraham, and in the book of Romans we are encouraged as new covenant people to walk in the footsteps of the faith of Abraham.

*"…walk in the steps of that faith of our father Abraham…"* – Romans 4:12

Give 10% to the living!

*"In the one case, the tenth is collected by men who die; but in the other case, by him who is declared to be living."* – Hebrews 7:8

*"…Jesus has become the guarantee of a better covenant"* – Hebrews 7:22

Jesus spoke about the issue of tithing…

*"Woe to you, teachers of the law and Pharisees, you hypocrites! You give a tenth of your spices—mint, dill and cummin. But you have neglected the more important matters of the law—justice, mercy and faithfulness. You should have practiced the latter, without neglecting the former."* – Matthew 23:23

## FOUR SCRIPTURAL BLESSINGS FOR TITHING

1. **Resources In God's House**
*(God's House is the place where you are spiritually fed)*
2. **Opening Of The Windows Of Heaven**
3. **Spiritual Pesticide** *(Rebuke the devourer)*
4. **You will be called "Blessed"**

If these scriptural blessings for tithing were available under the law, how much more blessing and glory will we see in our life as we allow the pattern of tithing to become a part of our life as new covenant believers! Moses experienced a fading glory, but we are walking into a realm of blessing where an ever increasing glory comes upon us in our finances.

God says He will open up the windows of heaven if we tithe. The tithe opens up a supernatural dimension of blessing over our lives. Finances will come to us right out of the *"open windows of heaven"* when we tithe. We won't be able to explain it, because it will be so supernatural.

*How does it work?*

We _____ our tithes.

We don't pray about what we are supposed to give, we are told through the scriptures that our tithes are equal to ten percent of all of our income. This is what we must pay to God. In this case we don't pray – we pay!!!

## ULTIMATE PURPOSE FOR TITHES

*"If therefore ye have not been faithful in the unrighteous mammon, who will commit to your trust the true riches?"* – Luke 16:11

*"No man can serve two masters: for either he will hate the one, and love the other; or else he will hold to the one, and despise the other. Ye cannot serve God and mammon."* – Matthew 6:24

God gives us the tithe with the obligation to pay it to him in order for us to walk in a level of faith which brings the blessing.  <u>This is a trust issue!</u>

## THE OFFERING – THE REALM OF FAVOR

*"And Jesus grew in wisdom and stature, and in favor with God and men."* – Luke 2:52

*"Give, and it shall be given unto you; good measure, pressed down, and shaken together, and running over, shall men give into your bosom. For with the same measure that ye mete withal it shall be measured to you again."* – Luke 6:38

*What is it?*

An offering is something that God requests and we give.

Offerings come in all shapes and sizes.  Sometimes they are little and other times they are huge, but the key here is that God sets the offering.  We don't decide the offering, God decides.

## A STORY OF TWO BROTHERS

*"And she again bare his brother Abel. And Abel was a keeper of sheep, but Cain was a tiller of the ground. And in process of time it came to pass, that Cain brought of the fruit of the ground an offering unto the LORD.  And Abel, he also brought of the firstlings of his flock and of the fat thereof. And the LORD had respect unto Abel and to his offering: But unto Cain and to his offering he had not respect. And Cain was very wroth, and his countenance fell."* – Genesis 4:2-5

God rejected Cain's offering because it wasn't what He asked for.

Offerings must be done in faith.

*"By faith Abel offered unto God a more excellent sacrifice than Cain, by which he obtained witness that he was righteous, God testifying of his gifts."* – Hebrews 11:4

How does faith come? How can we bring an offering in faith? Faith comes by hearing, and hearing by the Word of God. God always sets the offering. He speaks, we hear and we give our offerings in faith. (Romans 10:17)

We must listen to the revelation and then be obedient to it.

*"But be ye doers of the word, and not hearers only, deceiving your own selves. For if any be a hearer of the word, and not a doer, he is like unto a man beholding his natural face in a glass: For he beholdeth himself, and goeth his way, and straightway forgetteth what manner of man he was. But whoso looketh into the perfect law of liberty, and continueth therein, he being not a forgetful hearer, but a doer of the work, this man shall be blessed in his deed."*
– James 1:22-25

We must quicken to the revelation!

In Acts 4:32-5:6, Ananias & Sapphira tried to lie about the offering.

Acts 4 – these new covenant people tithed 10% and gave 90% offering. They put everything they had into the work of the Lord. They did this with gladness and a spirit of generosity.

Malachi 3:8 says that we can rob God of the offerings, not just the tithe. If we are not obedient to His voice, then we rob Him and we rob ourselves of His favor upon our lives.

The Intensified Glory Institute ———————— NOTES

*How does it work?*

We give offerings.

We don't pay them (they are not a repayment of a loan God has given to us, like the tithe), we always give our offerings.

The bible says that God loves a cheerful and prompt to do it giver whose heart is in his giving, so we should always bring our offerings to God with a happy heart and cheerful spirit. We need to put everything we are into our offerings!

The bible says that offerings will move men to give unto us. In other words, we will have favor with God and men as we pay our tithes and give our offerings.

*Do you see how the realms build upon each other?*

We establish ourselves in the blessings of God with our tithes, but then when we give our offerings it takes us to a whole new level of favor – not just with God, but now with men. The bible says that men will pour abundance into our laps (into our bank accounts, into our homes, into our ministries, etc.)

There are men and women right now that are assigned to pour financial blessing into your life! Begin believing and declaring the Word of God to release these divine finances into your lap! Lord, we release the men and women that are assigned to bring us wealth and prosperity. We declare that they will come and pour out such finances into our lives that we will be able to accomplish the vision You've given us!

*"Lord, as we give our offerings to you, we know that men are coming to us!"*

The bible says that a man's gift will make a way for him. Your giving will open up doors of opportunity, doors of expansion, doors of success and promotion. Your gift will open up doors of supernatural favor wherever you go.

The Intensified Glory Institute ———————————— NOTES

Right now let God show you what offering you're supposed to give, and as you give it to Him, begin to expect for men (or women) to show up in your life that will show you extreme favor!  Begin focusing on that scripture and declare the will of God – that there are men and women assigned to show you favor.  Right now they come in Jesus' name!

God loves our generosity.  It causes His glory to come with favor and with supernatural increase.

## THE SEED – THE REALM OF INCREASE

*"But this I say, He which soweth sparingly shall reap also sparingly; and he which soweth bountifully shall reap also bountifully.*

*[7] Every man according as he purposeth in his heart, so let him give; not grudgingly, or of necessity: for God loveth a cheerful giver.*

*[8] And God is able to make all grace abound toward you; that ye, always having all sufficiency in all things, may abound to every good work:*

*[9] (As it is written, He hath dispersed abroad; he hath given to the poor: his righteousness remaineth for ever.*

*[10] Now he that ministereth seed to the sower both minister bread for your food, and multiply your seed sown, and increase the fruits of your righteousness;)*

*[11] Being enriched in every thing to all bountifulness, which causeth through us thanksgiving to God.*

*[12] For the administration of this service not only supplieth the want of the saints, but is abundant also by many thanksgivings unto God."*

2 Corinthians 9:6-15

### *What is it?*

Seed is planted for a harvest. We set the seed according to our own desires. Within the scriptures sometimes the concept of "seed" is referred to as "Alms" – they are the same thing.

A seed is something that we have in our hand, which we know is not our harvest.

God gives us the ability to sow the seed or keep the seed. The choice is ours.

We receive increase in this realm according to the seed that is sown depending upon what we have purposed in our own heart to do. The seed is not set. This is amazing, because that means that the possibilities for our seed are unlimited. In other words, there is no limit to the supernatural harvest you can receive in this realm! Wow! *This is the realm of limitless increase!!!*

If we sow a generous seed we can expect God to give us a generous harvest! To the degree that we sow, is the same degree that we will begin to reap! God has promised us that as we sow into the heavens, He sows unto the earth.

Galatians 6:7-9

Acts 3:2 – Man asking for alms

Proverbs 19:17 – God repays "Supernaturally"

We sow and He multiplies it back to us. God never adds, He always multiplies!

God multiplies the fishes and the loaves! (Mark 6:32-44)

The largest loaf in the East was about 5 or 6 inches in diameter, about 1 inch thick or the size of three slices of our bread and more solid. This was not light bread. One man could easily eat one loaf; some could eat several loaves. Christ must have multiplied bread equal to 5,000 to 20,000 such loaves. He also multiplied the fish to as much as the 5,000 men could eat and had 12 baskets over. This was a creative miracle of increase and demonstrates that creation by the Holy Spirit is possible. Elisha by the gift of miracles multiplied bread from 20 loaves to feed 100 men (2 Kings 4:42-44). This power was manifested by an ordinary man. God wants to manifest this same glory through you and me!

### *How does it work?*

Every farmer understands that the more seed he plants in the ground, the more potential for increase he receives. A successful farmer will always plant seed in several fields. He knows that if his seed doesn't produce successfully in one field, than surely it will bring increase in another field of fertile soil.

We are coming into a day where the reaper WILL overtake the sower!

- Amos 9:13/John 4:35-38

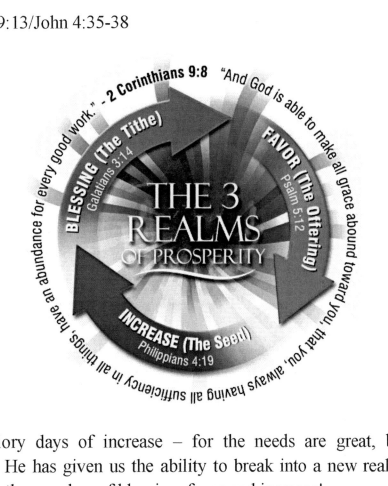

These are glory days of increase – for the needs are great, but our God is GREATER! He has given us the ability to break into a new realm of prosperity through these three realms of blessing, favor and increase!

## RECOMMENDED RESOURCES:

*CDs*

**Miracle Money**
By Joshua Mills
Distributed by PIP Media Group
P.O. Box 4037
Palm Springs, CA 92263

*Books*

**The Complete Personalized Promise Bible On Financial Increase**
By James Riddle
Published by Harrison House
P.O. Box 35035
Tulsa, OK  74153

All resources are available online at:
www.NewWineInternational.org

# The Intensified Glory Institute
# School of Signs & Wonders

# Lesson #11
# POWER IN YOUR HANDS

## Course I - Lesson 11

## POWER IN YOUR HANDS

**Objective:**  To understand the power of impartation and the ability that God has placed within each one of us to work miracles through our hands.

**Overview:**  Within this lesson we will search the scriptures and find out what the Word of God says about the power in your hands:

- What Do You Have In Your Hands?

- God Wants Your Hands

- Your Connection To Heaven

- Impartation Through "Laying On Of Hands"

- Facts On Impartation

## SCRIPTURES FOR MEDITATION:

□ 2 Timothy 1:6

□ 1 John 2:27

□ Mark 16

www.IntensifiedGloryInstitute.com

The Intensified Glory Institute ———————————— NOTES

# 🔒 HIDDEN REVELATION

As we worship the Lord, many times we will lift our hands into the air as an expression of our faith – but lifting our hands goes way beyond a simple gesture.

Medical science has found that the nerve endings to our eyes are placed in the palms of our hands. In some healing therapies they believe that many parts of the body are connected to the hands – this is why they may massage your hand to relax your eyes or even bring comfort to weary legs.

## WHAT DO YOU HAVE IN YOUR HANDS?

*"But the anointing which you have received from Him abides in you."*
– 1 John 2:27

In the Word of God there are ten meanings to lifting up our hands.

1. A sign of divine power (Exodus 9:29)

2. An act of faith (Exodus 17:12)

3. A habit in prayer (1 Kings 8:22, Psalm 28:2, Isaiah 1:15)

4. An act of seeking God (Psalm 68:31, Psalm 143:6)

5. An act of obedience (Psalm 119:48)

6. An act of worship (Psalm 134:2)

7. An act of creation (Isaiah 45:12)

The Intensified Glory Institute —————————— NOTES

8. An invitation (Isaiah 65:2)

9. An act of despair (Jeremiah 4:31, Lamentations 1:17)

10. An act of blessing (Luke 24:50)

## TAKE A LOOK AT YOUR HANDS!

God has given you these hands for a very specific reason.

Your hands are a point of contact to release the kingdom of God within you!

In Exodus 4, God asked Moses *"what do you have in your hand?"* because God wanted Moses to realize that His hands were overflowing and full of miracle working power!

The Intensified Glory Institute ———————— NOTES

## GOD WANTS YOUR HANDS!

We must give our hands to God in order for them to be filled with miracles.

Psalm 24:4 says in order for us to come into the dwelling place of God we must have *"clean hands"*. What does this mean? WE MUST BE PURE.

- Allow the power of God's Word to wash our hands clean (Ephesians 5:26)

- Repent of any wrong doing with our hands, including:

  - Abuse / Rage

  - Stealing / Robbery

  - Gluttony

  - Sexual Sins

  - Slander / Gossip (through written form), etc.

- **2 Corinthians 4:1-3**

- **Romans 12:1-2**

## YOUR CONNECTION TO HEAVEN

Your hands are your connection to heaven, and they are heaven's connection to earth! ***The anointing is caught, not just taught!***

### 2-WAY CHANNELS (in and out)

In worship we touch God _____ _____ → In worship we touch God ____ _____!

The Intensified Glory Institute ———————————— NOTES

## We Receive An Anointing By "Laying On Of Hands"

- **Isaiah 61:1** - Anointed to heal

## More Details:

- **Mark 16** - Heal the sick and cast out devils!

## When We Are Anointed <u>WE CAN DO IT!</u>

- **Proverbs 3:27**

## IMPARTATION THROUGH LAYING ON OF HANDS

Paul named *"laying on of hands"* as one of the basic fundamental doctrines a Christian should understand:

- Hebrews 6:1-2

Joshua was full of wisdom because Moses laid his hands on him!

- Deuteronomy 34:9

Elisha asked for an impartation from Elijah

- 2 Kings 2:9

Timothy received spiritual gifts by the "laying on of hands"

- 1 Timothy 4:14

Jesus healed a deaf man by laying his hands on him

- Mark 7:32-35

## FACTS ON IMPARTATION

- You can only impart what you possess!

- Through impartation you receive the "spark" to ignite the fire. (You must fan the flame!)

- When anointed hands are laid upon you, you are being directly hooked up to the power source of heaven! Receive what you need!

Question:

_____

_____

_____

Answer:

_____

_____

_____

_____

Question:

_____

_____

_____

Answer:

_____

_____

_____

_____

254

# About The Ministry Of
# NEW WINE INTERNATIONAL
## *Joshua & Janet Angela Mills*

**New Wine International, Inc.** is a 501(c)3 Federal Tax Exempt Non-Profit religious organization legally incorporated within the State of California.

**New Wine International** is also a registered non-profit charity within Canada.

## Mission Statement & Ministries:

*"Spreading the love and glory of God all over this world through praise, worship and revelation!"*

- Training the next generation of wonder-workers through seminars, church meetings, "Signs & Wonders Conferences" and **The Intensified Glory Institute**™

- Encouraging the spiritually seeking through SpiritSpa Weekends, revelatory teaching, and worship music available on CD, DVD and through books.

- Impacting the Media through Hollywood Invasions, television appearances and online presence.

- Making a global difference through ministry networking, missionary endeavors and overseas ministry outreaches.

## ABOUT JOSHUA & JANET ANGELA MILLS

An anointed Minister of the Gospel, Recording Artist, Keynote Conference Speaker and Author, Joshua Mills worships and preaches by standing within the cloud and ministering directly from the glory unto the people. He has written well over 600 songs and is known for his ability to lead people into spontaneous worship. Joshua has also been gifted to deliver a revelatory message of God's glory with understanding and impartation. During his services signs and wonders are commonplace with prophetic and accurate words of knowledge, manifestations of the heavenly realm and creative healing miracles. Janet Angela Mills ministers the Word of faith at Women's meetings and revival crusades in the nations. Joshua & Janet Angela Mills have appeared on many television programs – TBN, Miracle Channel, GodTV, Spike Network, 100 Huntley Street, Sky Angel, INSP Network, Daystar and in several magazine and newspaper publications. Joshua's songs and music continue to be played on both Christian and secular radio stations. Traveling all over North America and around the world, they have been creating a realm of glory wherever they go, with a message that *"praise changes the atmosphere."* In all of their meetings the sweet presence of Jesus Christ permeates the atmosphere and people's lives are changed forever. They currently reside along with their son, Lincoln, in London, Ontario, Canada as well as pursuing God's purpose and destiny for the Entertainment Industry in Southern California.

Joshua & Janet Angela Mills are ordained ministers with "Eagle Worldwide Ministries, Inc." and also with "City of Light, Inc.". They are also accountable spiritually, morally and doctrinally to a local church: **New Life Centre** · Pastors D. Karl & Cheryl Thomas · London, Ontario, Canada.

## WHAT WE BELIEVE

1. We hold as fundamental in everything that Jesus Christ is our only Lord and Savior. (John 14:6, Romans 10:9)

2. We believe that the Holy Bible is the inspired, infallible, and authoritative Word of God. The holy scriptures are the divine revelations given from God and received by man. The Bible is the supreme authority in all matters of faith and morals. It is the foundation for all decisions and is supreme in all manners in the Lordship of Jesus Christ. (John 16:13, 2 Tim. 3:15-17, 2 Pet. 1:21, 1 Thes. 2:13)

3. That there is one God, eternally existent in three persons: Father, Son and Holy Spirit. The Godhead is distinguishable but indivisible in essence; co-eternal, co-existent, co-equal in nature, attributes, power and glory. God is one undivided and invisible essence, yet with three eternal distinctions. (Deut. 6:4, Isa. 48:16, Matt. 28:18-19, Luke 3:22, John 14:16, Eph. 4:4-6)

4. The deity of our Lord Jesus Christ. The virgin birth, His sinless life, His miracles, His atoning death through His shed blood, His triumphant resurrection, His ascension to the right hand of the Father, and His personal return in power and in glory. (John 1:1-3,14-18, John 20:28-29, 1 Tim. 2:5-6, Phil. 2:6-11, Isa. 9:6, Col. 1:15-19)

5. Justification and sanctification of the believer through the finished work of Christ. Salvation is the free gift of God to man, separate from works and the Law, and is made operative by grace through faith in Jesus Christ, producing works acceptable to God . This salvation experience occurs when an individual confesses with his mouth that Jesus Christ is Lord and believes in his heart that God has raised Him from the dead. Sanctification is a definite, yet progressive work of grace, commencing at the time of regeneration and continuing until the consummation of salvation at Christ's return. (Romans 5:12-21, 10:9-10, John 3:16-17, 1 John 3:8, Phil. 3:12-14, 1 Cor. 1:30)

6. We believe in the present ministry of the Holy Spirit; which includes: the baptism in the Holy Spirit with signs following; His indwelling whereby the Christian is enabled to live a godly life; His divine healing for the physical ills of the human body, provided for in the atonement of Christ and wrought by the power of the Holy Spirit through believers; His supernatural gifting

www.IntensifiedGloryInstitute.com

and empowering of the church for its work, life and worship. (Luke 24:49, Acts 1:4-8, 2:1-4, 10:44-46, 1 Cor. 12,14)

7. Divine prosperity has also been provided by the atonement. True prosperity not only has to do with financial provision but a prospering of the soul as well. It is wrought by the power of God through the principles of tithes and offerings, sowing and reaping and numerous stewardship truths found throughout the Word of God. (1 John 2, 2 Cor. 8:9, Phil. 4:19)

8. In the spiritual unity of believers in our Lord Jesus Christ. (John 17:11, 21-23, Rom. 12:4-5, Eph. 4:11-16)

9. We believe in the personal return of Jesus Christ to receive His believers into heaven and eternal life. The time of His return is unknown; however, it may be at any moment. This is the glorious hope of all God's children. (John 14:1-3, 1 Thess. 4:13-18, James 5:7-8, Rev. 22:12-20)

## MINISTRY ENDORSEMENTS

*"When I first met Joshua Mills a number of years ago, I wondered, "Where has this man been hiding?" There was such a clear, profound, and powerful call of God on his life. I witnessed the manifestation of the glory of God through him in truly authentic, unusual, and awesome ways. What I love most about Joshua, Janet and Lincoln is their commitment to righteousness, integrity and humility. They are truly filled with the Spirit of faith, extremely gifted, and profoundly humble. It is apparent that they indeed love and exalt Jesus not only in public but when no one else is watching. Ron and I and our team at XP absolutely love Joshua and Janet Angela Mills… if you haven't had the pleasure yet of sitting under their ministry, you will too… you really will!"*
Patricia King,
Extreme Prophetic
Phoenix, Arizona
www.xpmedia.com

*"Joshua & Janet Angela Mills have one of the most unique and refreshing ministries that Joyce and I have ever experienced in our many years of ministry. God has joined our hearts together in a special way as we have ministered in their meetings, and they in ours, over the past number of years. We have witnessed manifestations of God's awesome glory in every meeting that reflect their pure hearts, absolute integrity and intimate relationships with the Lord. We highly recommend the Mills' ministry to all who are hungry for more of the presence and glory of God."*
Dr. A.L. & Joyce Gill, International Evangelists & Authors
Big Bear Lake, California
www.gillministries.com

*"I have had the honor and privilege to know Joshua and Janet for many years... I have been with them, traveled with them and have seen them ministering or just having fun together, and not once do they compromise the gospel... they truly are a gift from the Lord to share the signs, wonders and God's glory for such a time as this."*
Dr. Kaye Beyer, Evangelist
We Care For You Ministries
Tampa, Florida
www.wecareforyouministries.net

*"Joshua Mills is a living sign and wonder. He brings heaven to earth!"*
Sid Roth, Host
It's Supernatural Television
Brunswick, Georgia
www.sidroth.org

*"Joshua Mills is a man of integrity whom we are proud to be aquainted with. He is deep in the Spirit and in the Word. We are always honored for him to minister at our church."*
Pastors Richard & Dot Sarver, Senior Pastors
House Of Blessing Church and Healing Center
Leesville, Louisiana

*"Joshua & Janet Angela Mills are a complete package of Spirit and truth in both humility and integrity. Best of all is their friendship with God. I have been so blessed to minister with them and to get to know them."*
JoAnn McFatter, Prophetic Psalmist
Foley, Alabama
www.joannmcfatter.com

*"Joshua and Janet Angela Mills are some of the most refreshing ministers I know. I cannot think of a time when I have not been challenged, refreshed and left with my eyes more focused on Jesus after hearing them minister. Joshua also walks in one of the most accurate words of knowledge I have ever witnessed and I have personally seen the fruit of their ministry as people have been healed (physically) and set free in their meetings. What impresses me most about Joshua and Janet Angela Mills is not what I have seen them do in big crowds, but how I have seen them stop for individuals – or even go out of their way to find them – simply to share the gospel of Jesus Christ and lead people to the saving knowledge of who He is. They are gifts to the body of Christ and I love both their ministry and who they are as people."*

Faytene Kryskow, Bestselling Author & Ministry Leader
MYCanada, TheCRY & Fly High Ministries
Ottawa, Ontario, Canada
www.faytene.ca

*"I want to commend to you the ministry of Joshua and Janet Angela Mills. I have ministered several times with Joshua and have found his ministry to be very Christ centered and firmly grounded in God's Word. His preaching and teaching are very encouraging and edifying, building people's faith to receive from God's supernatural power. He not only moves in supernatural signs, wonders and miracles but is a true carrier of God's presence and has a heart like David. He is a man after God's own heart. He walks with true character, integrity and humility and I believe his ministry will be a tremendous blessing to you!"*

Matt Sorger, International Evangelist and Television Host
Matt Sorger Ministries, "Power For Life"
Seldon, New York
www.mattsorger.com

*"I have had the privilege of being in many of Joshua's services and also ministering with him. It is awesome how the power of God moves through him to bring the glory down in many unique ways. His words open up a new realm of power to the body of Christ. His wisdom goes way beyond his years."*

Joan Hunter, International Healing Evangelist

Joan Hunter Ministries
Kingwood, Texas
www.joanhunter.org

*"I highly recommend the ministry of Joshua & Janet Angela Mills. They both carry a very high level of signs and wonders on their lives, however, what I respect the most about Joshua and Janet is their grounding in the Word of God and in their character. They are real people and they are "solid" people. You will not regret receiving from their ministry as I know they will leave an amazing deposit of the Word and the Spirit of God with incredible supernatural demonstrations of the manifest glory and power of God in your midst!"*
Ryan Wyatt, International Evangelist
Abiding Glory Ministries
Knoxville, Tennessee
www.abidingglory.com

*"Joshua & Janet Mills are modern day "revelators" seeing and birthing the heart of God into you and I... they have showed me how to go into the Throne Room, no holding back, with open eyes and an open heart."*
Davene Fowler Garland, Worship Leader
Glenn Garland Ministries
Ashland, Virginia
www.glenngarland.org

*"Joshua Mills is an extraordinary man who lives in the Glory of God. His meetings with us have included the supernatural presence of God in very tangible ways. He is a joyful, humble, meek servant who ministers with authority, conviction and anointing!"*
Steve Long, Senior Pastor
Toronto Airport Christian Fellowship
Toronto, Ontario, Canada
www.tacf.org

*"The ministry of Joshua Mills is so unique and purposeful in that it takes you to a place in the presence of God that your faith will be stirred and increased to believe the impossible and you will experience the impossible."*
LaRue Howard, EMI Recording Artist & Pastor of Praise
FaithWorld Center of Orlando
Orlando, Florida

*"...The powerful manifestations and revelations of the glory that Joshua and Janet move in are a strong sign to us all that God is raising a Glory Generation that will reveal His heart to the world. Jan and I love them dearly and are privileged to know them as friends. We fully endorse their ministry!"*
Jeff & Jan Jansen
Global Fire Ministries
Nashville, Tennessee

*"Joshua & Janet Mills are the real deal. I minister often with them and always find both Joshua and Janet to walk in integrity, humility and the glory of God. Their ministry opens up a realm for people to experience God's life changing glory and power in their lives."*
Steve Swanson, Worship Leader
Friends of the Bridegroom Worship Ministries
Casa Grande, Arizona
www.fobworshipmin.org

*"I would recommend Joshua & Janet Angela Mills for any kingdom ministry that is called, committed and has a burden for souls. They are a precious gift to the body of Christ. Signs, wonders and miracles do flow in and follow their ministry. They will be a blessing to your ministry and cause it to go to another spiritual level!"*
Dr. Willett D. Mitchell, Senior Pastor
Judah Worship Word Ministries International
Fort Lauderdale, Florida

## MUSIC REVIEWS

**SpiritSpa: Instrumental Piano**

*"This CD is an ultra soothing experience in the presence of the Father. If you want to relax with God, get this CD and let the sounds wash over you in His presence of peace."*
T. Gaston, Austin, TX

*"...I love having SpiritSpa in my cd player and on my ipod. I can listen and work for hours at a time and never get tired of listening to Joshua play the piano. He does an amazing job of creating an atmosphere of worship and serenity... SpiritSpa is perfect to have on in the background, while you are reading, praying or working. I fully recommend SpiritSpa for every massage therapist as well as anyone else who is looking for music to aid in relaxation."*
Melody Barker, NCTM, LMT TX, LMT TN
Nationally Certified Massage Therapist
Nashville, TN

*"The piano is undoubtedly one of the most soothing instruments to calm one's nerves and musician Joshua Mills knows exactly how to do the job. His latest album of elegant piano compositions, "SpiritSpa," is not only delicate and dreamy but also a collection of wonderful piano ballads. The title says it all as this music does in fact belong in every spa across the country. His opening track, "Peaceful Soak," wraps you in beautifully written melodies... "Ascending & Descending" gives us something to listen to on one of those off days when we are all a little frustrated and need that one song that describes our day. Mills was also creative in the song names he chose as they very much reflect the ambiance of this album: "Glorious Horizon," "Fly," "Fragrant Oil," and "Heaven's Delight." Whether you just want to relax or hear some magnificent piano playing that soothes your body and soul, then "SpiritSpa" is for you."*
Shaun H.,
Radio Indy Reviewer Team
Encinitas, CA

264

## PARTNERS IN PRAISE

Partnership is not simply giving of your finances; it is more. When you become a **Partner in Praise** with New Wine International, you become an integral member of our outreach ministry team. In Matthew 28:19-20, Jesus issued the Great Commission and instructed us to *"Go into all the world..."* While you may never physically travel into the world to share the Gospel with those of other nationalities, you can still fulfill this mandate through your giving.

Partnership with this international ministry positions you to have global impact without ever leaving your hometown. When you give to New Wine International (NWI) through your prayer and financial support, you go with us wherever we are. When we are in Europe, you are there; when we are in the Arctic regions, you are there; when we are in Asia, you are there. Wherever we travel with the message of Jesus Christ - you are there, sharing in the glory with us!

**A "Partner in Praise" is a person who agrees to:**
1. Financially support the ministry of NWI
2. Pray faithfully for Joshua & Janet Angela Mills and the NWI Ministry Team as they carry the message of Jesus Christ around the world.
3. Pray for those who will receive ministry through NWI ministry events and resources.

Partnership is not only what you can do to help us, but also what we can do to help you. Becoming a **Partner in Praise** with NWI provides a covenant agreement between you and us. By being a **Partner in Praise**, you connect with the anointing and glory on this ministry. You will receive our continued prayer for you and your family and you will be linked with the unique anointing that is on this ministry for signs and wonders. In addition, we offer special benefits or "perks" for each partner option.

There are currently several ways to partner with NWI. You decide the membership level according to what the Lord has placed in your heart to do.

## PARTNERSHIP LEVELS

□ **SILVER**
**$30.00-$99.00 monthly gift, benefits\* include:**

Partners Package and regular mailings, along with email updates.
Prayer covering and prayer partnership (monthly phone call from NWI team member)
10% discount on NWI product at ministry hosted events
10% discount on NWI Conference registrations

□ **GOLD**
**$100.00-$499.00 monthly gift, benefits\* include:**

Partners Package and regular mailings, along with email updates.
Prayer covering and prayer partnership (monthly phone call from NWI team member)
15% discount on NWI product at ministry hosted events
15% discount on NWI Conference registrations

□ **PLATINUM**
**$500.00-$999.00 monthly gift, benefits\* include:**

Partners Package and regular mailings, along with email updates.
Prayer covering and prayer partnership (monthly phone call from NWI team member)
Personal phone call from Joshua & Janet Angela Mills during the year
20% discount on NWI product at ministry hosted events
20% discount on NWI Conference registrations

□ **DIAMOND**
**$1,000.00+ monthly gift, benefits\* include:**

Partners Package and regular mailings, along with email updates.
Prayer covering and prayer partnership
Monthly phone call from Joshua & Janet Angela Mills
25% discount on NWI product at ministry hosted events
25% discount on NWI Conference registrations
Receive one of the first copies of newest CD project

266

Name included in credits on CD (first CD released following partnership commitment)
CD personally signed by Joshua Mills
Beautiful certificate of appreciation and thanks

**If you would like to make a monthly partnership donation
or request more information, please call us toll-free at:**

# 1-866-60-NEW-WINE

*All discounts are applicable upon 4 months of consistent giving. Partners must call the ministry office when making conference registrations in order to receive the partnership discount. All partnership donations will receive a tax-deductible year end receipt in Canada and USA. New Wine International is a recognized Canadian not-for-profit organization and U.S. 501(c)3 non-profit religious corporation. All discounts, benefits and privileges subject to change without notice.